THE JESUS LIBRARY
Michael Green, series editor

The Teaching of Jesus

—Norman Anderson—

InterVarsity Press
Downers Grove
Illinois 60515

© *1983 by Norman Anderson*

Published in the United States of America by InterVarsity Press, Downers Grove, Illinois, with permission from Hodder and Stoughton Limited, England.

InterVarsity Press is the book-publishing division of Inter-Varsity Christian Fellowship, a student movement active on campus at hundreds of universities, colleges and schools of nursing. For information about local and regional activities, write IVCF, 233 Langdon St., Madison, WI 53703.

Cover illustration: Janice Skivington

ISBN 0-87784-926-9
ISBN 0-87784-933-1 (Jesus Library set)

Printed in the United States of America

Library of Congress Cataloging in Publication Data

Anderson, J. N. D. (James Norman Dalrymple), Sir,
   1908-
   The teaching of Jesus.

   (The Jesus Library)
   Bibliography: p.
   Includes index.
   1. Jesus Christ—Teachings.   I. Title.   II. Series.
BS2415.A48   1983   230   83-4312
ISBN 0-87784-926-9

---

17   16   15   14   13   12   11   10   9   8   7   6   5   4   3   2   1
96   95   94   93   92   91   90   89   88   87   86   85   84   83

THE JESUS LIBRARY
edited by Michael Green

The Hard Sayings of Jesus
F. F. Bruce

The Teaching of Jesus
Norman Anderson

Other books by Norman Anderson

Islamic Law in the Modern World
Islamic Law in Africa
Into the World
Christianity: The Witness of History
Christianity and Comparative Religion
Morality, Law and Grace
A Lawyer among the Theologians
Law Reform in the Muslim World
Liberty, Law and Justice
The Mystery of the Incarnation
Issues of Life and Death
God's Law and God's Love
God's Word for God's World

Editor's Preface

The Jesus Library will attempt in the eighties what the *I Believe* series achieved (at least to some extent) in the seventies. It was written by Christian scholars who were rooted both in the scriptures and the modern world. They took a fresh look at some important areas of Christian teaching which had been neglected or rejected in recent scholarly writing. Moreover, these books were written in such a way as to attract a wide general readership, keen to discover what the biblical material has to say on controverted issues of our day. This is precisely the aim of *The Jesus Library*.

The very centre of all New Testament enquiry is the person, the teaching, the death and resurrection of Jesus of Nazareth. The full deployment of Form and Redaction Criticism, coupled with the wide variety of presuppositions (often sceptical) brought by individual scholars, has sometimes in recent years had the effect of dulling the impact of Jesus or losing him beneath pages of learned footnotes. His very existence has been questioned, as has practically every one of his putative sayings, along with his incarnation, his miracles, his resurrection and the relation between the Jesus of history and the Christ of faith.

This series will re-examine various controversial aspects of the life and teaching of Jesus. It will seek to assess their authenticity and relevance. It is not a devotional series; neither is it intended for New Testament scholars alone. It is an attempt to allow the Jesus of whom the Gospels speak to emerge from the page and make his own impact on thoughtful people at the end of the twentieth century.

The present volume is contributed by Professor Sir Norman Anderson. He has dared to undertake one of the most difficult (because most comprehensive) themes one could possibly tackle – the teaching of Jesus. He is not a professional New Testament scholar, and that is a decided advantage, because it enables him to come fresh to the material without prior commitment to the entrenched positions on which so much professional work has concentrated. But although a layman in New Testament studies, he has written extensively on New Testament themes, and brings a wealth of experience to this book. He has been a missionary, a leading lawyer, a brilliant academic, an Islamic expert, and chairman of the House of Laity of the General Synod of the Church of England. He has run interdisciplinary seminars at the highest level on matters of Christian faith, and is an acknowledged expert on Christian ethics. I know of nobody with remotely comparable experience who has ever undertaken such a book. Indeed I can think of no book of such breadth on this subject since the days of T. W. Manson.

The reader will at once notice that Sir Norman concentrates on the Kingdom of God – its challenge, its life-style and its consummation – as the very core of the teaching of Jesus. That is not what is normally taught in church. Thus at once the book presents an implied critique and an explicit challenge. The author brings to a consideration of this central theme a variety of other qualities. His treatment is rooted in the text rather than in learned speculation. He is well versed in the literature of professional New Testament scholars. He comes to the subject with a freshness derived from another discipline. He deals powerfully with the personal and social ethics of the Kingdom. And the whole treatment is illuminated by the comparisons (and more often contrasts) which he draws with Islam.

Those who have absorbed this book will have a very good impression of the breadth and depth of the teaching of Jesus. The supreme need thereafter is to allow this understanding to penetrate our individual and corporate lifestyles.

Michael Green
Christmas 1982

Foreword

The teaching of Jesus stands on an Everest alone. No other teaching has had the same impact and influence, in countless lives and diverse cultures and ages. No other teaching has provoked so much change, or stirred so much debate. To sum up the teaching of Jesus in the scope of one comparatively slender volume is an almost impossible task. One way to tackle the problem would be to pick out certain major strands in his teaching and devote a chapter to each – with little or no obvious connection between them. Another would be to make a highly conjectural attempt to isolate the fundamental concepts which lie behind his teaching as a whole. But the plan I have adopted is to take what is almost certainly the basic theme which he proclaimed – the Kingdom of God – as the core or essence of his teaching, the thread that runs through all its varied facets, and the pattern that gives coherence to the whole.

After an introductory chapter which is concerned with how the Gospels came into being, the authenticity of the record they provide of the teaching of Jesus, and the way in which I propose to approach these records, the book falls into three almost equal sections. Part I (two chapters) is devoted to 'The Summons to the Kingdom' (together with virtually synonymous concepts such as 'Eternal Life' and 'Salvation'); Part II (three chapters) to 'The Ethics of the Kingdom'; and Part III (two chapters) to 'The Consummation of the Kingdom'.

There are, almost inevitably, certain consequential disadvantages in adopting any such method. Some aspects of Jesus' teaching have, no doubt, received less prominence than they properly deserve, or may even have been omitted altogether. But I have tried to cover as wide a spectrum as possible and to allow his teaching to speak for itself, rather than force it into any preconceived mould. I hope, too, that the very numerous quotations I have made from the Gospel records will ensure that passing reference, at least, has been made to many points in addition to the primary emphasis for which I have cited these reported 'sayings'. Finally, a short epilogue summarises the implications of a unifying theme which in some ways runs parallel to the Kingdom in the teaching of Jesus – namely, the fatherhood of God – which has, of course, surfaced in chapter after chapter in one context or another, but to which no special or separate section had previously been devoted.

My own academic subject is law rather than theology, and I have tried to write for as wide an audience as possible, with the needs of students (whatever their discipline) primarily in mind. Chapters 4–6 are, in substance, based on three public lectures on 'The Ethics of Jesus' which I gave, in February 1982, in the Faculty of Theology in the University College of Cardiff, to whose courtesy I want to pay a warm tribute. Biblical quotations throughout the book are predominantly from the New English Bible or the New International Version; but I have occasionally had resort to the Jerusalem Bible or to a translation of my own.

Chapter
1

Introduction

This book represents an attempt to summarise, and in some measure to discuss, the teaching of Jesus as this is set forth in the Gospels. It makes no pretension (except in a few passing comments) to identify or assess the Gospel tradition which lies behind the text of the evangelists. This would necessarily involve 'the patient process of scrutinising each verse in the Gospels in turn, both by itself and in relation to all possible parallels' (Barrett, *Gospel Tradition*, p. 102), which would clearly be impossible – and indeed intolerable – in a book like this. In any case, such a task would be beyond my expertise. It is true that a lawyer is not wholly unaccustomed to having to weigh up and assess the often conflicting evidence put forward by expert witnesses from almost any discipline; and the more knowledge and understanding of the points at issue he himself has, or can acquire, the better. But he must stick to his last and not assume the role of an expert witness himself.

Even continually to summarise, on point after point, the rival opinions of those New Testament scholars whose works I have read, and then explain in detail why I would opt for one view rather than another, would entail writing a very different, and vastly longer, volume. So I have kept such discussion to a minimum.

Naturally enough, the fact that I have studied and taught Islamic law for many years has aroused my interest in the remarkable similarities, as well as the outstanding differences, between the nature, origin and development of the authoritative sources of Christianity and Islam, and the way in which Christians and Muslims have come to regard and interpret them. So I have made some comments in the present chapter, and very occasionally elsewhere in the book, about points that seem relevant – whether by way of illustration or contrast – to the study of the New Testament. But first we must turn our attention briefly to the sort of teacher Jesus himself was.

Jesus as Teacher

Throughout the greater part of the New Testament, the major emphasis falls on 'the Christ event' as this is summed up in the mission, passion, resurrection and exaltation of Jesus. To the apostolic Church he was primarily their risen Lord, now enthroned as Messiah and Son of God, whose return in glory, salvation and judgment they were eagerly awaiting. But while these titles are by no means absent from the body of the Gospels, the predominant title by which he was addressed during his earthly life was undoubtedly 'Teacher'. This is usually rendered by the Greek *didaskalos*, or in Luke sometimes *epistatēs*, both of which terms are normally translated 'Master' in the Authorised Version. But behind both of them stands the Hebrew 'Rabbi', which is at times retained both in the Greek and in English versions, and was the usual form of respectful address to a distinguished teacher. It is a striking fact that Jesus is addressed as 'Teacher', under one or other of these titles, over fifty times in our Greek Gospels.

And what a teacher he was! He seems to have been equally at home preaching in a synagogue or speaking in the open air; debating with religious leaders or talking about the things of God with simple villagers. He could catch and hold the attention of a large (and sometimes hungry) crowd, or give intimate instruction to a little band of committed disciples. He was perfectly at ease when dealing with a secret enquirer like Nicodemus, a Roman governor like Pilate, a Samaritan woman whom he met at a well or a weeping prostitute who approached him in a Pharisee's house. He could speak with gentle forgiveness to self-confessed sinners, and with stern denunciation to religious hypocrites.

Most of his teaching seems to have been extempore, arising from personal encounters, challenges or questions, and from the varied occurrences and situations of everyday life. As a consequence it was not set out – normally, at least – in a systematic form. He was clearly a master of what William Barclay terms 'the unforgettable epigram', the sort of phrase that 'lodges in the mind and stays there, refusing to be forgotten'; of 'the thought provoking paradox', that appears incredible but makes people go on wondering whether it may not be true; and of 'the vivid hyperbole', that deliberately uses an over-statement to arrest the hearer or to emphasise a point (*Mind,* pp. 99f.). In many of these cases either the twinkle in his eye or the tone of his voice would have conveyed to his hearers the sense in which he used the words. But above all else the stories or parables in which so much of his teaching was couched stand out as unique – not as a method of teaching *per se* (particularly to the young, the simple and all those who think more readily in the form of mental pictures than the written word) but for their vividness, variety, quality and content.

His teaching proves that he was acutely observant of the processes of nature, the details of village life and the minds and hearts of men. Though he had never graduated from one of the rabbinical schools he had a profound knowledge of the Old Testament Scriptures, which he had clearly pondered deeply. He had no doubt learnt the rudiments of such study in the local synagogue school; but his understanding of the true meaning of these Scriptures and their application to his own mission must have come directly from 'Abba' – the heavenly Father whom he grew to know, commune with and depend on so intimately. It is, perhaps, noteworthy in passing that in both teaching and controversy Jesus at times used the techniques of *reductio ad absurdum* ('but that would lead to an absurdity'), *argumentum ad hominem* ('but even on your own princ-iples ...'), *argumentum a fortiori* ('but how much more then ...') and reasoning by analogy, in ways that not only brought home the truth to his hearers but reduced hostile critics to silence, as W. A. Curtis has shown (*Teacher,* pp. 79ff.). Not infrequently he expressed his teaching in a poetical or rhythmical form which must have been easy to remember or even to memorise. And he spoke not only as a teacher but also as a prophet, in which capacity he was widely acclaimed.

It is when we turn to the records of his teaching which have come down to us that a comparison with the oral and written sources on which Muslims rely as authoritative seems to me much more apposite than the references to local or ethnic traditions and folklore which are sometimes made in relation to the Gospel tradition. The difference is that both Christians and Muslims regarded the subject matter as sacred and authoritative – for Muhammad longed that the Arabs should have an equivalent of the Jewish and Christian Scriptures.

The 'Book' and the 'Traditions' of Islam

The basic sources of Islam are its Holy Book, the Koran (properly, *Qur'ān*) and the Practice (*Sunna*) of its Prophet – as these are established by those traditions (*aḥādīth*) about him which have come to be accepted as authentic. Orthodox Muslims believe that the Koran was written from eternity in Arabic in heaven and was 'sent down' to Muhammad – little by little, as occasion required – through the agency of the archangel Gabriel. In the traditional view Muhammad could neither read nor write. This is the sense in which the adjective '*ummī*' (Koran 7:156 and 158) has been commonly understood, although the term might be regarded as roughly equivalent to the description of Jesus in John 7:15 as *mē memathēkos*, 'unlearned' in any rabbinical school; and Richard Bell has made out a strong case for his conviction that Muhammad himself wrote, and on occasion revised, some of the units (pericopae) of which the Koran is made up (*Introduction*, pp. 17ff., 82ff.). However this may be, some of the 'revelations', we are told, were jotted down by his Companions on 'palm-leaves, leather, and the ribs and shoulder-blades of animals'. For the most part, however, they were committed to memory – a feat that was facilitated by the rhyming and rhythmical prose in which they were composed – and were probably not extensively committed to writing, and certainly not collated as a book, until a few years after his death.

There has been much speculation about the way in which the different units of revelation were arranged in *sūras* or chapters – in some cases, in Bell's opinion, by Muhammad himself (*Introduction*, pp. 82f.). Muslims commonly assert that the first Recension of the text of the Koran as a whole was made by Zayd ibn Thābit very soon after the prophet's death – and it is generally accepted that a collection of relevant material must have been made substantially at this date. But it is a mistake to imagine that this was the only collection, for a number of different collections co-existed in early years, some of which attained the status of metropolitan Codices (Jeffery, *Qur'ān*, pp. 103ff);[1] and it was only under the third Caliph, 'Uthmān, that an official Recension was made and sent to the great metropolitan centres, with orders that all other Codices or collections should promptly be destroyed (Jeffery, *Qur'ān*, p. 94).

A considerable body of variant readings from these Codices were in fact collected by Arthur Jeffery 'from the grammatical, lexical and masoretic literature of later generations which still remembered and discussed them'; and he even discovered and published the only known surviving example of an Arabic work on this subject – the *Codex Book* of Ibn Abī Dāwūd. In addition, until 322 A.H. (i.e. year of the Hijra, or 'Hegira')[2], the official text was itself purely consonantal and devoid of any diacritical marks, so an enormous number of variant readings and interpretations of this text have been recorded (Jeffery, *Qur'ān*, pp. 97f.)[3] There were also disputes about such matters as the positioning of the signs used to mark verse endings. So, although it is true that today the Kūfan text of Ḥafs is accepted almost everywhere in the Muslim world, the claim commonly made by Muslims that they have the *ipsissima verba* of what Muhammad actually said, without any variant readings, rests upon an ignorance of the facts of history.

Much of this will represent comparatively familiar ground to students of the Greek New Testament, with its variant readings and its regional textual traditions, represented by the

Alexandrian, the Western, the Caesarean and the Byzantine Codices. What is absent is anything comparable to 'Uthmān's attempt to impose an official text and to exclude variants. Even more germane to our subject, Arthur Jeffery has stated that 'Perhaps even in the Prophet's own life-time there were certain members of the community who took an interest in "collecting" the pronouncements of their Prophet. In this there is nothing unusual. It was precisely this that in the earliest Christian community provided those collections of "Sayings of Jesus" that we find among the basic material of the Gospels' (*Qur'ān*, p. 92). Thus the discrete units of material which can still be distinguished in the text of the Koran (easily enough, very often, by reason of a change in the prevailing rhyme) correspond to the less clear-cut pericopae (or individual units of tradition) discerned in the Gospels by 'Form-criticism' (see below), while the first major collection of material, attributed to Zayd ibn Thābit in the Caliphate of 'Umar, may be compared with suggestions about written sources of our Gospels such as a 'proto-Mark', 'proto-Luke' or the 'Logia' ('Sayings') ascribed to Matthew (see below). To the way in which the text of the Koran was committed to memory we must soon revert.

The most obvious difference in the nature of the Koran and the New Testament is not only that the former is a unit, composed by (or, in the Muslim view, 'sent down to') one man, but that it is all represented as the direct speech of God. Fragments of history, legislation, moral teaching and the musings of Muhammad are uniformly introduced by the imperative 'Qul' or 'Say'. In consequence it is, strictly speaking, improper to assert that anything in the Koran represents the 'teaching of Muhammad', since everything is regarded by Muslims as coming directly from Allāh. It is only when we turn to the traditions that we find material that may properly be cited as teaching ascribed to the Prophet. Even among these *aḥādīth* (which towards the end of the second century of the Hijra came to have an authority second only to that of the Koran), there were in fact a few *aḥādīth qudsiyya* ('sacred' traditions) that are regarded as statements made by God himself which were not, for whatever reason, incorporated in the Koran. But the vast majority of the innumerable traditions, which in due course flooded the market, ostensibly represent some episode in the life of Muhammad in which he spoke, acted or behaved in a way which came to be considered by the orthodox as inspired in content (in contra-distinction to the strictly verbal inspiration which they ascribe to the Koran).

At first these traditions were handed down quite casually – and, as is freely admitted, frequently invented; but when the *Sunna* (words or example) of the Prophet came to have normative authority, jurists and traditionalists alike began to insist on a chain of narrators (reaching, in theory, right back to one of Muhammad's Companions), each of whom had memorised the teaching or incident and had been duly authorised by the one from whom he received the report to narrate it to others. Every tradition, therefore, came to consist of two parts: the *isnād*, or chain of narrators, followed by the *matn*, the story they attested.

That the Koran, as we have it, substantially represents the revelations which, Muhammad claimed, had been vouchsafed to him through Gabriel, no one (Orientalists included) seems seriously to doubt, whether these revelations were compiled from written records or the memory of those to whom they were originally declared. The traditions, on the other hand, were not reduced to written form until about the middle of the third century of the Hijra.[4] Each individual tradition (*hadīth*) represents a wholly distinct unit, the authenticity of which could be, and was in fact, minutely scrutinised – so much so that al-Bukhārī, the author of the earliest of those six 'reliable' collections of traditions that are regarded as authoritative by most Sunnī Muslims, is said to have examined some 600,000 and to have recorded only about 7,000.

Unhappily, however, this minute scrutiny was confined to the *isnād* or chain of narrators: whether their characters and powers of memory commanded respect; whether each of them *could* have received it from his predecessor; and whether the chain went back without a break to a contemporary of the Prophet. No such attention was given to the *matn* or subject matter – regardless of the fact that a very respectable *isnād* could well be transferred from one tradition to a story which was clearly invented in response to conditions or matters of debate which prevailed only at a considerably later date. As a consequence it has even been asserted that *none* of the traditions that have come down to us can be accepted as indubitably authentic[5] – although very few scholars would take quite such an extreme view.[6] The fact remains, however, that even Muslim scholars often take a radically different attitude to the authenticity they ascribe to the Koran and to individual traditions.

Criteria of Authenticity

Certain 'criteria of authenticity' (all of which could be applied to the chain of narrators rather than the substance of the relevant traditions) were commonly recognised by Muslim traditionalists. Thus they made a distinction between traditions classified as *mutawātir* (that is, handed down by many distinct chains of narrators), *mashhūr* (handed down by some three lines of narrators) and *khabar al-ahad* (depending on only one witness, or one chain of narrators). By these criteria various traditions came to be classified as 'genuine', 'mediocre', 'weak', etc.; but it is noteworthy that some vital principles in Islamic law depend, in the final analysis, on the veracity and dependability of a single witness. Much of this bears a *certain* resemblance to the criteria of 'Multiple Attestation' and 'Multiple Forms' which are applied by some New Testament scholars to sayings of Jesus attested by more than one source or occurring in more than one form. It would certainly be widely accepted that the presence of these criteria provides plausible *positive* evidence that the teaching or incident concerned was relatively central to the *kerygma* (proclamation), but not that their absence should be regarded as constituting any negative proof of inauthenticity (cf. Marshall, *Historical Jesus*, pp. 203f.).

Muslim scholars were also compelled to grapple with the

problem of *faskh* (abrogation) when two verses in the Koran, two traditions, or a Koranic text and a tradition seemed to be contradictory. Most of them acknowledged the possibility of one authentic revelation completely superseding an earlier one; but they came to the sensible conclusion that, wherever possible, a general statement of principle should be regarded as qualified, rather than abrogated, by a more detailed instruction that appears to contradict it. This seems to me much more reasonable than the way in which some biblical scholars all too easily assert that two authors or editors contradict each other, or even that one writer contradicts himself. Another sound principle observed by Muslim scholars is that an obscure text must always be interpreted in the light of those perspicuous verses which they regard as 'the mother of the Book', and not *vice versa*. Bible students have commonly insisted on a similar principle.

Happily enough, no Muslim scholar that I know of has adopted the *negative* use of the criterion of Dissimilarity or Discontinuity by means of which some New Testament critics feel bound to question the authenticity of every 'saying' of Jesus for which *any* authority also exists either in Judaism or in the apostolic Church. It is manifestly absurd to imagine that Jesus never endorsed anything from the Scriptures or traditions of Judaism, or that the Church which confessed his name never echoed any of his teaching; so the negative application of this criterion would inevitably filter off the vast majority of his teaching and, by retaining only what is unique rather than characteristic or central, completely distort the whole picture (cf. Marshall, *Historical Jesus*, p. 201). But this is not to call in question the positive application of this criterion to underline, for example, the unique distinctiveness of his use of the term 'Abba' as an address to God in prayer or of the word 'Amen' as an introductory formula for a particularly emphatic statement (Jeremias, *Prayers*, pp. 54–65). Many other examples could be cited of points characteristic of the life and teaching of Jesus, as these are depicted in the Gospels (cf. Moule, *Phenomenon*, pp. 52–7, 63–8), which run directly counter to the accepted rabbinic tradition, on the one hand, and can certainly not be credited to the apostolic Church, on the other.

The Gospel Traditions

But how were the traditions which lie behind our Gospels preserved, and what can we say about how the Evangelists used them? To discuss these very complex and controversial subjects in detail would go far beyond the scope of this chapter. We have seen, however, that in Islam part of the substance of the Koran was written down during the lifetime of Muhammad and the remainder committed to memory; that a compilation of some sort was made very soon after his death; and that the official Recension under 'Uthmān was promulgated within about twenty years (30 A.H.). The traditions (which were not, in fact, in rhyming prose) were, by contrast, passed on by word of mouth for a very long time, and the vast majority even of those which came to be accepted as authentic were not recorded in writing for two or three centuries. This is why in this case Muslims came to insist on an ostensibly reliable chain of narrators.

In Christianity, by contrast, the Bible represents the only authoritative written source of revelation, and there is nothing that is really comparable with Islam's collections of authoritative *ahādīth*.[7] Some of the Epistles, written little more than twenty years after the Crucifixion, represent the earliest documents in the New Testament that have come down to us as such. The Gospels, for their part, certainly include units of traditional material, some of which were probably not reduced to writing for some years; but the so-called 'Tunnel Period' is measured in terms of a very few decades rather than centuries, and is comparable to the period before the promulgation of the official version of the Koran rather than the books of traditions. Some of the teaching of Jesus may well have been jotted down in his lifetime (cf. Ellis, *Prophecy*, pp. 243–7);[8] and the emergence of the first of our Gospels in its present form was probably preceded not only by the written records to which reference is made in Luke 1:1, but by the 'Logia' ascribed by Papias to Matthew, by the hypothetical document usually referred to as 'Q', and possibly by a 'proto-Mark' or 'proto-Luke' (or first drafts of the Gospels concerned).

It can, in any case, be stated with confidence that the theology of Paul, for example, did not rest exclusively on personal revelations from the heavenly Lord, or on his own processes of thought, but also on objective truths about the teaching, life, and resurrection of Jesus that had been transmitted to him by eye-witnesses (cf. 1 Cor. 15:1–11). Nor can there be any doubt that the original disciples must have been repeatedly questioned about these subjects by a series of converts, and that their replies – and the information they gave in their preaching and teaching – must have assumed a more and more stereotyped form. The assertion that the primitive Church was 'not interested' in details about the life and teaching of Jesus of Nazareth is incredible to any student of Islam. It is true that the Epistles, which were largely written in response to specific problems, do not include many such references, but the Gospels themselves belie any such idea (Stanton, *Preaching*, p. 186). Almost certainly a catechesis for catechumens must soon have taken shape; and this would have been largely based on the mission and teaching of Jesus.

Dr Harald Riesenfeld and Dr Birger Gerhardsson have asserted that Jesus taught his disciples to commit both his teaching and his interpretation of the episodes of his life to memory, and that the apostles were the authoritative guardians and expositors of this sacred tradition. But there is no evidence in the Gospels that Jesus urged his disciples to learn his teaching by heart in the way which has been so widespread in the history of both Judaism and Islam; and a comparative study of the Gospels seems to prove that the historical tradition was more concerned with the substance of Jesus' teaching than with canons of verbal exactitude. R. T. France has, however, aptly remarked that 'an exaggerated case is not necessarily wholly false', and that

What Gerhardsson has done is to call our attention to the

milieu in which the Christian Church began its life, that of
Palestinian Judaism. The early Christians may not have
copied every detail of the rigid technique of transmission in
the scribal schools, with their use of trained memorizers of
tradition and their insistence on verbal accuracy, but if we
want an analogy for the nature of the early Christian
tradition it would seem *a priori* more likely that we shall find
it in this milieu than in Greek and oriental folk-literature.
The historical context in which the Church originated places
the presumption in favour of an accurate transmission of
sayings-material unless there is evidence to the contrary
('Authenticity', p. 121).

It is in this context that France quotes the comment of W. D.
Davies (who does not by any means accept Gerhardsson's
views without criticism) that 'we can no longer doubt that the
process whereby the Christian tradition was transmitted is to
be largely understood in the light of Pharisaic [or, I might add,
Islamic] usage in dealing with Oral Tradition'. Elsewhere
Davies remarks that 'it is highly pertinent to note that there was
frequent intercourse between figures such as Peter, and other
apostolic guardians of the tradition, and Christian communities in various places, so that the transmission and development of the tradition was not unchecked'. So his conclusion is
that it is 'far more historically probable and reasonably
credible, over against the scepticism of much form-criticism,
that in the Gospels we are within hearing of the authentic voice
and within sight of the authentic activity of Jesus of Nazareth,
however much muffled and obscured these may be by the
process of transmission' (Davies, *Setting*, pp. 446, 417, 480). In
my opinion his final caveat is somewhat unnecessarily
guarded, since much of Jesus' teaching must have been
comparatively easy to remember in considerable detail – vivid
parables, striking aphorisms and hyperboles, controversies
with critics, and comments on miracles, for example.

We must refer to the individual Gospels shortly. What we
need to remember at this point is that the first of our Gospels
almost certainly appeared before the end of the fourth decade

after the death of Jesus, if not earlier, and was most probably in the process of compilation for several years before that. If we date 1 Corinthians about 55 A.D., then some three hundred or more people who claimed actually to have seen the risen Christ were alive at that date, and several of the leading apostles were still living (cf. 1 Cor. 15:6). Thus a large number of eye-witnesses of the ministry of Jesus, and some of the apostles themselves, were in a position to contribute to, verify and check the oral traditions available to the Evangelists and also, as many would claim, at least the earliest of the written records. It stands to reason, too, that the apostles, as the leaders of what was then regarded as a heterodox Jewish sect, would have wished to exercise considerable control over such traditional teaching, whether oral or written.[9]

The fact is that in the primitive Church 'the pattern of teaching' (which would comprise both that of Jesus himself and that of the apostles) was taken very seriously indeed. Thus in Romans 6:17 Paul writes: 'Thanks be to God! You were indeed slaves of sin, but from your heart you gave your obedience to that pattern of teaching to which as slaves you were handed over.' On this verse C. K. Barrett comments that the reference is to 'Christian (not Pauline) teaching', and that one would expect 'the doctrine to be handed over ... to the hearers, not the hearers to the doctrine. But Christians are not (like the Rabbis) masters of a tradition; they are themselves created by the word of God, and remain in subjection to it' (Barrett, *Romans*, p. 132). It is clear, moreover, that while Paul claimed that his own teaching was authoritative, he was careful to make a distinction between this and actual statements by Jesus himself (cf. 1 Cor. 7:10, 12). So the suggestion that declarations made by Christian prophets in the name of Jesus as revelations from the heavenly Lord were included in the traditions as sayings of the earthly Jesus runs directly counter to the available evidence.

Our Four Gospels

Any study of the first three Gospels reveals a marked similarity in their general historical structure and, in parts, their detailed wording. Sometimes, indeed, two of them agree even more closely in content, style and vocabulary compared with the third; at others one Gospel stands alone; and there are many differences in detail. These factors lie at the root of the 'Synoptic Problem'. The most widely accepted solution today is that both Matthew and Luke had access to Mark and to a hypothetical documentary source, 'Quelle' (mostly made up of teaching material), which accounts for material common to these two Gospels and absent from Mark; and that both Matthew and Luke also had independent sources of information ('M' and 'L'). But this theory is not without serious difficulties. So some scholars would eliminate the need for 'Q' by postulating that Luke had access to Matthew as well as Mark (or even by supporting the earlier belief in the priority of Matthew), while others believe that Luke (or 'proto-Luke') was available to Matthew. Until comparatively recently, again, it might fairly be said that scholars turned to the synoptic Gospels for historical data and to John for theological reflection.

But theories about dating the fourth Gospel in the second century have had to be drastically revised by the discovery of Rylands Papyrus 457 (Roberts, *Fragment*). What is more, it has now been recognised that, even if this Gospel was the last to be written (which is by no means certain), it unquestionably rests on some very early, vivid and essentially Palestinian traditions. John Robinson (in his *Redating*) seems to me at the least to have shown that what he terms the current 'critical orthodoxy' regarding the dates to be ascribed to the Gospels rests on very tenuous foundations. A major factor in this critical consensus is an explicit or implicit denial that Jesus could or did prophesy future events (which seems to me a wholly untenable assumption), and an implicit assertion that the fall of Jerusalem, as depicted in Matthew and Luke, could not have been described in that way by any student of both the

Old Testament and the contemporary scene possessed of any degree of prophetic insight (Dodd, 'Fall', 69-83). It is interesting, too, to note that John 21:24 would seem, on the surface at least, to express the assurance of a possible editor, or the Johannine circle, that it was 'the disciple whom Jesus loved' who 'attests' [present tense] these things', who was at least the substantial author, and whose testimony they knew to be true. This represents the only (and distinctly remote) parallel in the Gospels to the chain of narrators on which Muslim scholars came to insist when the oral narration of the traditions had extended over a *very* much longer period.

Robinson expresses his conviction that, whereas epistles were written for specific occasions, 'gospels were essentially for continuous use in the preaching, teaching, apologetic and liturgical life of the Christian communities. They grew out of *and with* the needs. One can only put approximate dates to certain states or stages ... And at any stage in this development one must be prepared to allow for cross-fertilisation between the on-going traditions' (*Redating*, p. 94; his italics.). This statement does not necessarily involve any suggestion that the apostolic Church *invented* traditions to meet their needs (as is, unquestionably, true of many of those traditions about Muhammad which – in spite of their chains of narrators – clearly refer to situations and subjects which were alien to his life and environment). The Gospels certainly include traditional material which was *selected* because of its relevance to the life and problems of the Church; but they also preserve many traditions which seem positively to have forced their way through a soil that was by no means congenial to them, for no discernible reason other than that they were a faithful record of what Jesus had actually said and done (Moule, *Phenomenon*, pp. 62, 65).

Each Evangelist clearly made use of the traditions that were available to him – including, in some cases, one or more other Gospels. Much can, indeed, still be said in support of the once widely accepted view that Matthew's Gospel includes a collection of the sayings of Jesus which may well have been made by, or under the aegis of, the apostle himself, and that the

Gospel as such was addressed to, or emerged from, a predominantly Jewish-Christian community; that Mark's Gospel owes a great deal to Peter's preaching, and was written primarily for the Church at Rome; that Luke's Gospel was written by a close associate of Paul, that he supplemented his sources (both written and oral) by information he had gleaned directly from eye-witnesses, and that he designed his Gospel chiefly for converts and enquirers in the Gentile world; and that John's Gospel rests primarily on the testimony of 'the beloved disciple' and was addressed to Greek-speaking Jews.

'Form-criticism' has plausibly suggested that many of the units in the tradition emerged as such in the course of the preaching and teaching of the apostolic Church; and 'Redaction criticism'[10] has rightly emphasised the fact that each of the Evangelists wrote with a theological purpose and arranged his material accordingly – with the three Synoptists all following the same broad chronological sequence. M. R. James and others have shown, moreover, the enormous gulf that separates the 'Apocryphal Gospels'[11] from those that were accepted as 'Canonical'; and the Church all down the centuries has been immeasurably enriched by having this four-fold portrait of Jesus. It is in the light of the basic consistency of this portrait that so much in the Apocryphal Gospels can confidently be rejected.

The Actual Sayings of Jesus

It cannot, of course, be claimed that Jesus' teaching has been preserved in his *ipsissima verba*. To begin with, he did not normally teach in Greek, but Aramaic; so the problems inherent in any translation inevitably arise. Again, our records clearly amount to no more than the barest summary of teaching, both public and private, spread – it would seem – over some three years. As an itinerant preacher he no doubt often returned to the same subjects, and he must have used the same illustrations, metaphors and similes in a number of different contexts and for a variety of purposes; so it would be exceedingly rash to assume that sayings recorded in one Gospel or setting which resemble those in another must always be based on the same originals. In many cases, however, the context makes it clear that the Evangelists have reported the same tradition in different words – sometimes adding explanatory phrases which we today might put in footnotes, and sometimes telescoping, combining or rewording their material.

In these circumstances it is often little more than a matter of conjecture, or at best individual judgment, which of the Evangelists has, in each instance, come closest to the original. 'There are no hard and fast laws of the development of the Synoptic tradition', E. P. Sanders has concluded:

> On all counts the tradition developed in opposite directions. It became both longer and shorter, both more and less detailed, and both more and less Semitic. Even the tendency to use direct discourse for indirect . . . was not uniform in the Synoptics themselves. For this reason, *dogmatic statements that a certain characteristic proves a certain passage to be earlier than another are never justified* (*Tendencies*, p. 272; his italics).

In a book like this it would clearly be impossible, therefore, to discuss each 'saying' on its merits; so I shall in the main take quotations from one or more of the Gospels as seem best to serve my purpose. There is much truth, I think, in T. F. Torrance's statement that the 'direct impact' of the teaching of Jesus, as recorded in our four Gospels,

> has been somewhat blunted through a changed attitude to the sheer majesty of the Gospels that has resulted from historio-critical research. The intention of this research has been to confront us today across the centuries with the original Jesus, undiluted and unobstructed by layers of interpretative material with which His teaching has so often been overlaid. Yet it is now more and more evident that the claims we have made for 'assured results' from our critical

research are greatly exaggerated. In our interpretative criticism we have been insufficiently aware of ... hidden assumptions and presuppositions ... so that too often we ourselves are guilty of overlaying the original Jesus with distorting interpretations of our own. Now that these hidden assumptions are being brought to view and are found again and again to be untenable ... many of us are increasingly convinced that the traditional form of the Gospels commands our acknowledgment, making us want to listen to the Words of Jesus in the coherent patterns in which they were set in the formation of the evangelical tradition (*Christ's Words* [Foreword]).

My own view can be summarised very briefly. In some cases the teaching of Jesus as recorded in the Gospels is very close indeed to a translation of his *ipsissima verba* – particularly in certain aphorisms and other striking sayings, in some of his parables, and in characteristic phrases. In other cases I myself make a distinction between what I would term the *ipsissimus sensus* of his teaching, on the one hand, and his *ipsissima vox*, on the other.

Under the first of these terms I would put the numerous contexts in which the Evangelists seem to be recording in their own words some specific (but probably now no longer precisely identifiable) saying of Jesus, while I would apply the concept of the authentic 'Voice' of Jesus, for example, to those passages in John's Gospel where it is impossible to draw any firm line between words the Evangelist attributes to Jesus himself and his own reflections on their meaning and application. This can be seen clearly enough in his third chapter: but an outstanding instance of what I have in mind is presented by the Farewell Discourses. Several cross references to teaching recorded in the synoptic Gospels can be found in these chapters, so it seems likely that the Evangelist (whoever he was) filled out these fragmentary traditions with teaching which 'the disciple whom Jesus loved' could vividly remember and the way in which he had come to understand what his Master had taught. I realise, of course, that the line between what I have termed the *ipsissimus sensus* of Jesus' teaching and what I prefer to think of as his authentic 'Voice' may be nebulous, but I believe the distinction is not without meaning.

Finally, I myself firmly believe that the biblical authors were not left to their own unaided resources. Just as the authentic prophets of the Old Testament could say 'Thus saith the Lord', and just as Jesus himself clearly recognised the divine authority of the Jewish Scriptures, so it stands to reason, I think, that God would not have left mankind without authoritative written testimony about the supreme revelation of himself in Jesus and the New Covenant he inaugurated. It was thus that Paul could affirm in his Epistles that the Gospel he proclaimed had been divinely revealed to him (Gal. 1:11f.), that he could pass on to his converts 'the word of the Lord' (1 Thess. 4:15) and could give instructions in his name (2 Thess. 3:12).

At first sight, of course, the Evangelists seem to represent a different case – making use, as they did, of oral tradition, written sources and the memories of eye-witnesses (including, it may very well be, their own). It seems clear, in any case, that the tradition was formulated at a time when *many* eye-witnesses were still alive; that it is distinctly possible that early drafts of one or more of the Gospels actually ante-dated the Epistles; and that even the final product may well have been promulgated under apostolic auspices. My point in this particular context is not, however, the reliability of the sources that were available to the Evangelists but my belief that the Holy Spirit not only recalled to the conscious memory of eye-witnesses material imprinted on their subconscious minds, but also guided the Evangelists in selecting the material they used – and, indeed, in adapting its wording, explaining its meaning and, at times, adding their reflections on it – in a way which conveys to us a record of the teaching of Jesus which commands both our confidence and response.

As one reviews the teaching of Jesus as a whole it becomes increasingly clear that its central focus is on the Kingdom of God: its proclamation, its ethics and its consummation. So the rest of this book will be arranged accordingly.

Part I

The Summons to the Kingdom

Chapter
2

The Proclamation and Nature of the Kingdom

The Background to the Teaching of Jesus

When Jesus began his ministry of teaching and preaching in Galilee, his very first proclamation, we are told, was: 'The time has come; the Kingdom of God is upon you; repent, and believe the Gospel' (Mark 1:14). It was, indeed, this announcement that the Kingdom of God[1] was so imminent that it could, in a real sense, be said to have already come (Matt. 12:28), which represents the sum and substance of Jesus' message and mission. Nor does he seem to have felt it necessary to define or explain the term, for he was not only re-echoing – in virtually identical words, but with a radically new significance – the basic challenge of John the Baptist (Matt. 3:2), but using a phrase which encapsulated the essence of the proclamation of the Old Testament prophets, the vision of the Jewish apocalyptists, and the teaching of the Qumran community.

This concept of the kingship or rule of God has been described as both the integrating centre of the teaching of Jesus and the bond that binds the Old and New Testaments together (Bright, *Kingdom*, p. 197). It is true that the specific phrase 'the Kingdom of God' is not found as such in the Old Testament (although it is all but used several times in the book of Daniel); but the idea behind it constantly recurs. Numerous passages speak of God as the King who in fact reigns, even now, not only over Israel but the whole world, although the prophets were deeply conscious that this was not what seemed to be the case either in Israel, with her disobedience and frequent apostasy, or – still less – in the surrounding nations (cf. Cranfield, *Mark*,

p. 64). So other passages foretell a day when he will 'become King' and rule absolutely, in mercy and in judgment, not only over his covenant people but with universal sway. It is significant in this context that the Hebrew word *malkûth* primarily denotes reign, dominion, or kingly power, and only secondarily the realm over which this is exercised.

The Old Testament prophets were not content, however, to proclaim the sovereignty of God as a transcendental fact which would be universally manifested at the end of the age; for they persistently called on kings, priests and people to abjure the worship of any other god, to repudiate the moral evil of their ways, and to live as loyal subjects of their true King. They insisted that God is at all times active in history – planting and uprooting, casting down and building up; for the transcendent Lord is continually 'visiting' his people.

Yet beyond all these temporal and imminent visitations the prophets discerned and predicted an eschatological 'Day of the Lord' when he would break into history, in a spectacular way, finally to destroy evil and establish his reign of salvation and peace. Characteristically, the prophets often found it difficult to make any sharp distinction between the activity of God in the present or immediate future and his ultimate, eschatological intervention – for even this was conceived in earthly terms. The Hebrew prophets never accepted the Greek concept of a 'bodiless, non-material, purely "spiritual" redemption'. It was not the disembodied spirits of individual men and women but human society, and even nature itself, which must share in God's new creation (cf. Ladd, *Presence*, pp. 59f.).

It is their concern with the activity of God in history, and with the response of their contemporaries to his warnings and promises about the future, that chiefly distinguishes the prophets of the canonical Old Testament from the apocalyptists of the inter-testamental Apocrypha. During the Babylonian exile Israel had been purged from her previously endemic idolatry and polytheism, and those Jews who participated in the restoration under Ezra and Nehemiah had, as a community, renounced apostasy and set themselves to obey the law of their God. Yet the blessings that would, it was promised, follow repentance had not in fact been experienced.

Instead, Israel had been dominated by a succession of largely foreign rulers, and the voice of authentic prophecy had fallen silent. It was to this enigma that the inter-Testament apocalyptists addressed themselves. At times they resorted to the expedient of projecting themselves into the past and re-writing history in the guise of prophecy. But their salient characteristic was a profound pessimism, and even impassivity, in regard to the wrongs and sufferings of this present evil age,[2] and a concentration on dreams and revelations of the eschatological future – often by means of the literary device of visions attributed to some outstanding figure of the past.

The Qumran community greatly prized some of these apocalyptic writings, but had its own distinctive stance. Like all its Jewish contemporaries, it made no claim to have received the direct word of authoritative prophecy; but it did believe that the Holy Spirit had given special illumination to its founder, the Teacher of Righteousness, to discern the true meaning of the 'Mysteries' hidden in Habakkuk and other prophetic writings. The sect looked forward to the advent of the prophet promised in Deuteronomy 18:18, and meanwhile held strictly to 'the whole counsel of the Torah'.[3]

It was at this juncture that John the Baptist appeared. Whether he had ever been a member of the Qumran community is a matter of speculation; but both the style and the content of his ministry were such that Israel as a whole soon came to realise that at last another true prophet had been raised up. His primary message to all was that the 'Kingdom of God' was literally at the very door. He was neither a political revolutionary nor an apocalyptic visionary who foretold salvation for Israel and doom for her oppressors. Instead, he demanded that those who had been content to claim that they had Abraham for their father should make an act of public repentance, and that men of every class and calling should prove the sincerity of their repentance by the ethical quality of their lives. But his ministry, he insisted, was only in preparation for the coming of one much mightier than he, who would baptise not with water but with the Holy Spirit and with fire, gathering the 'wheat' into his granaries of preservation and blessing but burning up the 'chaff' in the fire of destruction. In other words, God was about to intervene and visit his people, with messianic salvation and eschatological judgment, through the agency of this Coming One.

The Mission and Message of Jesus himself

This proclamation of the imminence of the Kingdom and the accompanying summons to repentance were, as we have seen, repeated by Jesus in virtually the same words, but with a ring of authority and an expansion of meaning that were startlingly new. Where John had called on men to 'prepare a way for the Lord' because the Kingdom of God was 'upon them', in the mouth of Jesus these words had an enhanced urgency and dynamic quality. In Mark's formulation this is made clear by the preface: 'The time has come' (Mark 1:14); for Jesus did not merely insist, like John, on the imminence of the coming Kingdom, but asserted that the divine visitation had actually begun and that God was already, here and now, visiting his people.

In Matthew's Gospel Jesus is reported to have stated this explicitly when, after an exorcism which aroused considerable controversy, he said: 'if it is by the Spirit of God that I drive out the devils, then be sure that the kingdom of God has already come upon you' (Matt. 12:28). And in Luke's Gospel, where the first recorded incident in Jesus' ministry is his sermon in the synagogue of Nazareth, we are told that he read from the scroll of Isaiah:

The Spirit of the Lord is upon me because he has anointed me;
He has sent me to announce good news to the poor,
To proclaim release for prisoners and recovery of sight for the blind;
To let the broken victims go free,
To proclaim the year of the Lord's favour.

and then said: 'Today in your very hearing this text has come true' (Luke 4:21).

The significance of these statements is, I think, obvious. The difference between the message and mission of John and Jesus, as Günther Bornkamm puts it, is 'like that between the eleventh and the twelfth hours. For Jesus calls: the shift in the aeons is here, the Kingdom of God is already dawning ... It is happening now in Jesus' words and deeds' (Bornkamm, *Jesus*, p. 67). What perplexed John in Herod's dungeon, and even made him wonder whether he had been right in identifying Jesus as the Coming One of whom he had prophesied, was that the 'shift in the aeons' was so little in evidence, and that the irruption of eschatological judgment and messianic salvation was so delayed. But Jesus simply told John's disciples to go back and tell John what they had seen: 'the blind recover their sight, the lame walk, lepers are cleansed, the deaf hear, the dead are raised to life, the poor are hearing the good news' – and to add (either in gentle reproof or sympathetic encouragement): 'happy is the man who does not find me a stumbling-block' (Matt. 11:4-6; cf. Luke 7:22f.). The signs of the advent of the Kingdom were there, but not its full realisation.

As has often been emphasised, Jesus is recorded as ending the quotation from Isaiah 61 in the synagogue of Nazareth with the words 'to proclaim the year of the Lord's favour' without adding 'a day of vengeance for our God' – for the time for the eschatological consummation of the Kingdom was still future. Warnings of judgment to come were not absent from Jesus' teaching; but the predominant emphasis was on the messianic salvation which had already begun in both works and words of power. The preaching of the Gospel was not simply new teaching: it was the proclamation of a new event. 'God is no longer waiting for men to submit to his reign but has taken the initiative and invaded history in a new way' (Ladd, *Presence*, p. 144). This was why Jesus said to his disciples, on another occasion: 'happy are your eyes because they see, and your ears because they hear! Many prophets and saints, I tell you, desired to see what you now see, yet never saw it; to hear what you hear, yet never heard it.' (Matt. 13:16f.; cf. Luke 10:23f.)

It is noteworthy that Matthew reports this saying in the context of his collection of 'parables of the Kingdom', and even places it between the parable of the Sower and its interpretation; so it is to these parables of the Kingdom that we must soon turn. But it is pertinent at this point to note that the words recorded in Luke 16:16: 'Up to the time of John it was the Law and the Prophets: since then, the good news of the Kingdom of God is being preached, and everyone [or 'all who will' (Knox)] is forcing his way in', presumably correspond with the mysterious statement in Matt. 11:12 which is usually translated (as in the text of the N.E.B.) 'Ever since the coming of John the Baptist the kingdom of Heaven has been subjected to violence and violent men are seizing it.'

As a number of commentators[4] have observed, however, the Greek word here translated 'subjected to violence' can be construed as representing the middle voice just as well as the passive, and translated 'the kingdom of heaven has been forcefully advancing, and forceful men lay hold of it' (cf. N.I.V. text; N.E.B. and R.S.V. marginal readings) – which would represent a reference to the dynamic power of the good news of the Kingdom proclaimed by Jesus, and the imperative need for a decisive response, or whole-hearted reaction, on the part of those who hear it. Thus W. Hendriksen translates this verse: 'the Kingdom of heaven is pressing forward, and vigorous men are eagerly taking possession of it' (*Matthew*, pp. 488f).

The crucial importance of this saying is thrown into sharp relief by the statements which precede and follow it in Matthew's record. Jesus introduces the preceding verse with his authoritative 'Amen, I say to you', and declares that 'of all the children born of women, a greater than John the Baptist has never been seen; yet the least in the kingdom of heaven is greater than he is.' He then follows his reference to the dynamic power of the Kingdom that he proclaimed with the words: 'Because it was towards John that all the prophecies of the prophets and of the Law were leading: and he, if you will believe me, is the Elijah who was to return. If anyone has ears to hear, let him listen!' (Matt. 11:13–15. J.B.). It would scarcely be possible to make it clearer that in the person and message of Jesus a new aeon had dawned.

Yet there was also what seems at first sight to have been a diametrically different strain in his teaching about the Kingdom, for he explicitly taught his disciples to pray: 'your kingdom come, your will be done, on earth as it is in heaven' (Matt. 6:10). At Nazareth, moreover, his implicit proclamation of his messianic mission was immediately followed by fierce opposition (Luke 4:28), and we are specifically told by Mark that 'he could not do any miracles there, except to lay his hands on a few sick people and heal them. And he was amazed at their lack of faith' (Mark 6:5f.). As time went on the hostility of the Jewish leaders seems to have become more and more intense, in spite of the fact that he made no explicit messianic claims in his public ministry – chiefly, it would seem, because they would have been understood in terms of the national deliverer or Davidic king they expected the Messiah to be. Instead, it was to the prophecies about the Suffering Servant in the book of Isaiah that he appears increasingly to have turned as foreshadowing his mission; and it was almost certainly Isaiah 53:10ff. that he had in mind when he told his disciples that 'even the Son of Man did not come to be served, but to serve, and to give his life as a ransom for many'.[5]

He also spoke explicitly, in Matthew 24 and parallel passages, about the Parousia and the end of the age. Thus there is a close resemblance between the statement recorded in Mark 13:26: 'At that time men will see the Son of Man coming in clouds with great power and glory', and that in which he responded to the High Priest's explicit question before the Council 'Are you the Messiah, the son of the Blessed One?' by his reply: 'I am.[6] And you will see the Son of Man seated at the right hand of God and coming with the clouds of heaven' (cf. pp. 154, 182f. below).

The Mystery or Secret of the Kingdom

How, then, is this apparently ambivalent view of the Kingdom – as present but yet still to come, as active but not yet consummated – to be explained? It seems clear that it is this very ambivalence which represents the key to an overall understanding of the 'parables of the Kingdom';[7] namely, the 'mystery' or 'secret' of the Kingdom of God which Jesus said had been divinely given to his disciples rather than to the people as a whole, in the Marcan version, or the different aspects of that basic mystery (when the same Greek word is used in the plural) in Matthew 13:11 and Luke 8:10. Cranfield understands this mystery as

> the secret that the Kingdom of God has come in the person and words and works of Jesus. That is a secret because God has chosen to reveal himself indirectly and in a veiled way. The incarnate Word is not obvious. Only faith could recognise the Son of God in the lowly figure of Jesus of Nazareth. The secret of the Kingdom of God is the secret of the person of Jesus (*Mark*, p. 153).

Tasker brings out the ambivalence of the concept even more explicitly when he comments on the Matthean version:

> There are *mysteries* about the kingdom of heaven, and they arise because the kingdom is present but not yet in its fullness, and because the King is at the moment rejected and humiliated so that the glory that belongs inherently to Him and which will one day be visible to all is at present obscured. The inauguration of the kingdom by Jesus the Messiah has already taken place, but the outward signs of its presence are as yet very few. It is here, but not with irresistible power. Men can and do reject it. Indeed, it can be accepted only by those whose hearts have been made ready to receive it, just as seed can produce a crop only when it is sown in ground prepared for its fertilization. That is the essential point of the parable of the sower (*Matthew*, p. 137).

Many scholars today make a sharp distinction between the parables of Jesus and the explanation of them that he is recorded as having given to his disciples. The parables themselves, it is generally agreed, are 'a fragment of the original rock of tradition . . . Everywhere behind the Greek text we get glimpses of Jesus' mother tongue', and 'the pictorial element of the parables is drawn from the daily life of Palestine'. They so clearly 'reveal a definite personal character, a unique clarity and simplicity, a matchless mastery of construction' that 'the conclusion is inevitable that in reading the parables we are dealing with a particularly trustworthy tradition, and are brought into immediate relation with Jesus' (Jeremias, *Parables*, pp. 11f.). When it comes to the interpretation of the parable of the Sower, on the other hand, Joachim Jeremias, like C. H. Dodd and others, concludes that this does not represent the words of Jesus himself, but 'is a product of the primitive Church which regarded the parable as an allegory, and interpreted each detail in it allegorically' (*Parables*, 79). This is partly because, ever since Adolf Jülicher, it has not only been axiomatic to many New Testament scholars that allegorical interpretations of the parables were, in the past, both excessive and fanciful, but 'that the parables in general *do not admit of this method at all*, and that the attempts of the evangelists themselves to apply it rest on a misunderstanding (Dodd, *Parables*, 13; my italics).'

Now it is true that an allegory, as 'an extended or continued metaphor' (O.E.D.), is often an artificial story, devised specifically as a medium for instruction, in which every detail may well have a distinctive and relevant meaning. A parable, by contrast, is normally a story told in the form of a simile drawn from everyday life, which is intended to drive home one basic lesson, and in which some, at least, of the other features or details are included simply to make the picture life-like. But Cranfield has justly insisted that 'it is a mistake to make this into a hard and fast rule. To maintain a rigid distinction between parable and allegory is quite impossible in dealing with material originating in Hebrew or Aramaic, languages which have only one word to denote both things' (*Mark*, p. 159).

Elsewhere he states that the key to the understanding of the term *parabolē* in the synoptic Gospels is the use of the Hebrew word *māšāl* in the O.T. and (together with its Aramaic equivalent) in Rabbinic literature, and observes: 'The term *māšāl* covers a wide range of meanings including the ethical maxim, the short sentence of popular wisdom, proverbs generally, by-word, taunt-song, oracle, riddle, comparison, allegory, fable, in addition to what is meant by "parable" in the strict sense' (*Mark*, p. 148). And the equivalent word in Arabic (*mathal*) has a similar range of meanings.

Thus it is wholly arbitrary to assume that the parables of Jesus were always simple illustrations which conveyed moral and spiritual truths which were so easy to understand that his disciples did not need any special instruction about their meaning (Tasker, *Matthew*, p. 136). The major problem that confronts us, then, is why, at a certain stage in his ministry, Jesus for a time appears to have confined his public teaching to parables (Mark 4:11, 33f.). On the face of it, it would seem intolerable to believe that Jesus would have couched his teaching in 'riddles'[8] with the deliberate intention that the majority of his hearers would not be able to understand their inner meaning. But in this context a number of points should be noted.

First, when Jesus said that it was to his disciples that the 'secret' of the Kingdom of God had been 'given' (Mark 4:11) the concept 'that God's thoughts and ways are not men's, but that they are his secret, which is not obvious to human wisdom but which he may reveal to those whom he chooses', was familiar to everyone who listened attentively in the synagogue. There was an Aramaic word at hand to express it – the word used in Daniel – and it is probable that that word *rāz* is behind *mystērion* here (Cranfield, *Mark*, p. 153). The word *mystērion*, moreover, was widely used by Paul for something that can be comprehended only by divine illumination, or was previously hidden but now revealed.

Second, we read in Mark 3:6, 22 about plots against Jesus and the attribution of his supernatural power to 'the prince of the demons'. So, instead of broadcasting divine truths to those who would have rejected or distorted them out of hand, he told them vivid stories about which those whose hearts God touched could ask him questions.

Third, the supreme 'secret' of the Kingdom – and of all his

teaching – was Jesus himself. As E. C. Hoskyns put it, the understanding of these parables 'depends upon the recognition of Jesus as the Messiah and upon the recognition of the Kingdom of God which is breaking forth in his ministry' (*Riddle*, p. 188). Jesus himself stated categorically in Matthew 11:27 that 'No-one knows the Son except the Father, and no-one knows the Father except the Son and those to whom the Son chooses to reveal him.' But he immediately followed this seemingly exclusive declaration with the open invitation: 'Come to me, all you who are weary and burdened, and I will give you rest. Take my yoke upon you and learn from me'. So the use of parables served to sift the hostile, proud and indifferent from those who wanted to learn and understand.

We read, indeed, that 'With many such parables he would give them his message, so far as they were able to receive it'; so it was presumably open to them to join the inner band of disciples to whom 'he explained everything' (Mark 4:33f.). But to have hawked about theological mysteries to those whose hearts, far from being prepared, were wilfully closed, would have been to go right against the proverb (quoted by Jesus himself in Matthew 7:6) 'Do not give dogs what is holy; do not feed your pearls to the pigs: they will only trample on them . . .'

Thus all the Synoptists record that Jesus began his explanation of the parable of the Sower – the archetypal explanation of a particular parable that has come down to us as a key to that of parables in general – by an explicit reference to the mystery of divine revelation as a gift from God (Matt. 13:11; Mark 4:11; Luke 8:10). In Matthew's account he then told them that to one who acts on the revelation he has, more light will progressively be given, while light that is refused or disregarded fades away (Matt. 13:12). In all the synoptic Gospels, moreover, he explains his resort to parables by a reference (whether longer or shorter) to the words of Isaiah 6:9 and 10. In Matthew 13:14f. (and again in Acts 28:26f.) this passage is quoted in the Septuagint version rather than the Masoretic text: that is, that the prophet was to tell the people 'You will hear and hear, but never understand; you will look and look, but never see. For this people has grown gross at heart; their ears are dull, and their eyes are closed. Otherwise their eyes might see, their ears hear, and their heart understand, and then they might turn again, and I would heal them.'

In the Masoretic text of Isaiah 6:9 and 10(a), on the other hand, the prophet is not told to address the people in the indicative tense as a prediction of what would happen, but in the imperative ('Hear and hear again, but do not understand; see and see again, but do not perceive') and is instructed to 'Make the heart of this people gross; make their ears dull and close their eyes'. The N.I.V. follows the Masoretic text in its translation of Isaiah 6 but puts the Septuagint version in a footnote, while the N.E.B. follows the Septuagint in Isaiah, as well as Matthew and Acts. The much briefer reference in Mark 4:12 and Luke 8:10, together with a longer quotation from the same passage in Isaiah in a different context in John 12:39ff., are in each case closer to the Masoretic text.

Perhaps the chief difference between the Evangelists is that in Matthew the reference to Isaiah's prophecy about people's inability to understand is introduced by the Greek word '*hoti*' (which either means 'because' or serves to introduce a quotation in direct speech), while in the other three Gospels we find '*hina*' (which in classical Greek means 'in order that', or may be used in sub-classical Greek for 'so that'). Thus the prophecy is cited in John to explain the persistent rejection of Jesus by his fellow countrymen, and particularly their religious leaders, in the words:

> For this reason they could not believe, because, as Isaiah says elsewhere, 'He has blinded their eyes and deadened their hearts, so they can neither see with their eyes, nor understand with their hearts, nor turn – and I would heal them'. Isaiah said this because [or 'when'] he saw Jesus' glory and spoke about him (John 12:39f.).[9]

We must always remember, however, that the difference between the two versions (the Masoretic text and the Septuagint) would not have seemed nearly so great to the

Hebrew mind as it does to us, for in Semitic thought what actually happens in any situation can readily (and with no sense of incongruity) be ascribed to the divine decree, without in any sense lessening the human responsibility of the persons concerned. It is clear from this passage and from Romans 9–11, for example, that to both John and Paul God is the 'First Cause' of all that happens in the history of salvation. So it is significant that John ends this very passage by observing: 'For all that, even among those in authority, a number believed on him, but would not acknowledge him on account of the Pharisees ...', while Paul's conclusion is that 'God has consigned all men to disobedience, that he may have mercy upon all' – followed by a doxology (Rom. 11:32–6).[10] On this whole subject W. L. Lane aptly comments:

> The citation of Isa. 6:9 does not mean that 'those outside' are denied the possibility of belief. It indicates that they are excluded from the opportunity of being further instructed in the secret of the Kingdom so long as unbelief continues. That the Kingdom has come in an initial phase in the presence of Jesus can be discerned only through faith, which is to say by the grace of God. Jesus' presence, therefore, means disclosure *and* veiling; it releases both grace *and* judgment (*Mark*, p. 159).[11]

Some Parables of the Kingdom

The major concentration of 'parables of the Kingdom' in any one chapter is in Matthew 13. Two of these seven parables, those of the Sower and the Mustard Seed, are also found in both Mark and Luke, while one, that of the Yeast, is again recorded in Luke. The other four are peculiar to Matthew. The parable of the Sower (Matt. 13:3ff. and parallels) depicts the widespread proclamation of the good news of the Kingdom, but emphasises the fact that, in this present age, the self-same message largely depends for its effects on the qualities and circumstances of the hearers, and on the degree of their response. But it should be noted in passing that Jeremias (*Parables*, pp. 11f.) points out that the farmer in this parable was not negligent in sowing his seed on soil where villagers had walked or thorns were growing, since he intended to plough the seed in, and the thorns up, afterwards; and the underlying limestone would scarcely show at this stage. Thus what 'appears to the western mind as bad farming was simply customary usage in Palestine, where sowing habitually preceded ploughing, not *vice versa*'.

The parable of the Tares or 'Weeds' (Matt. 13:24ff.) fills out this parable in two ways; it teaches us, first, that it is not only the farmer who sows, for an 'enemy' also sows a very different sort of seed in the same ground; second, that the wheat and the weeds must be allowed to grow together during this life, and the separation between them must be left until the day of judgment. This last point is re-emphasised, but in a different pictorial setting, in the parable of the Dragnet (Matt. 13:47ff.)

The simile of agricultural growth is further expanded in the parable of the Mustard Seed (Matt. 13:31f., and parallels) and in the little parable, peculiar to Mark, about the way in which seeds grow in general (4:26ff.). The latter complements the parable of the Sower by insisting that, whereas growth depends on man's response and human farmers plant and water, it is God alone who ultimately produces the harvest (cf. 1 Cor. 3:7), while the parable of the Mustard Seed emphasises the fact that the Kingdom, even if now barely visible, will have a glorious manifestation at the Parousia. It is to this same fact that the parable of the Yeast (Matt. 13:33) also witnesses by means of a different simile, for the way in which the kingly reign of God now permeates its environment invisibly will then be openly revealed.

Finally, the remaining parables in Matthew 13 – those of the hidden Treasure and the magnificent Pearl (vv. 44ff.) – do not, of course, mean that the Kingdom can be purchased or selfishly hoarded for oneself alone,[12] but that its intrinsic value, both in eschatological prospect and present possession, is such as to transmute any conceivable cost into joyful gain.

There are other parables of Jesus recorded in the New

Testament which were explicitly designed to throw further light on the meaning and nature of the Kingdom. Some of these will be discussed when we consider Jesus' ethical teaching; but others demand a brief mention here, since they illustrate the fundamental basis of entrance into – and exclusion from – the Kingdom as it now exists, and also give us at least a hint of what its future consummation will mean. In this context it is important always to bear in mind G. E. Ladd's admirable summary of the meaning of the 'mystery' of the Kingdom – a phrase to which several references have already been made; for he insists:

> That the Kingdom was to come in apocalyptic power was no secret; it was affirmed also by orthodox Jewish theology. The mystery is a new disclosure of God's purpose for the establishment of his Kingdom. The new truth, now given to men by revelation in the person and mission of Jesus, is that *the Kingdom which is to come finally in apocalyptic power, as foreseen in Daniel, has in fact entered into the world in advance in a hidden form to work secretly within and among men* (*Presence*, pp. 224f; his italics.).

We shall begin this second series of parables of the Kingdom with that of the Unmerciful Servant (Matt. 18:23ff.). This seems to preclude any possible misunderstanding of the parables of the hidden Treasure or the magnificent Pearl by making it abundantly clear that the only possible way into the Kingdom is through a full and free forgiveness. The 'debt' of our sins is almost inconceivably great, however little we realise this, and any idea of repayment, or self justification, is wholly impossible; so our only hope is to throw ourselves on the mercy of the King, whose compassion is always available to those who seek it in genuine contrition. But the repentance of the servant in the parable was bogus, as he immediately showed by refusing an almost identical appeal for compassion from a fellow servant (who owed him an incomparably smaller debt) with callous brutality. Many of the details in this parable have, of course, been taken from contemporary practice to make the story life-like, and should certainly not be allegorised; but the basic teaching is inescapable (cf. pp. 108, 9 below).

Much the same lesson lies at the heart of the parable of the Workers in the Vineyard (Matt. 20:1–16), in which there are, I think, two salient features: the compassion of the landowner for those who stood about in the market place with no work, no livelihood and no purpose in life; and the manifest inequity, by market standards, of the pay the different labourers received at the end of the day. It is this second point which provides the primary lesson of the parable: that entrance into the Kingdom is not a matter of human desert at all, but is based solely on the grace or unmerited favour of God. In so far as our enjoyment of it rests on us at all, it is not the length or diligence of our work that counts, but rather whether we open our mouths wide enough to receive all he longs to give us (cf. Ps. 81:10).

Further Parables of the Kingdom

We must now turn to a trilogy of parables which, in Matthew's account, immediately follow the questioning of Jesus' authority by the chief priests and elders recorded in Matthew 21:23ff. At first sight his reply to their question 'By what authority are you doing these things?' is an outstanding example of the principle that the best form of defence is attack, for he asks them a counter question ('Whence was John's baptism, from heaven or from men') which they dare not answer. But they must have understood the implication of his reply: namely, that John's ministry was by the authority of God, and so too was that of the One to whom John had borne his humble witness. The majority of the Jewish leaders were, however, as unwilling to acknowledge or accept the one as the other.

The first of these three parables is that of the Two Sons (Matt. 21:28ff.). Here the second son clearly depicts many of the religious leaders of the day, with their reverent speech and ready acknowledgement of their ceremonial duties, all too often characterised by dismal failure in genuine devotion or practical obedience. They were those who 'said, but did not do'; they did not hesitate to 'tie up heavy loads and put them on men's shoulders', but they themselves were 'not willing to lift a finger to move them' (cf. Matt. 23:4). The first son, on the other hand, was rude and defiant to his father – two cardinal sins against contemporary mores and the Mosaic law; but 'afterwards he changed his mind and went'.

I well remember, when I was a missionary in Egypt, hearing about a preacher who recounted the first part of this parable, asked his audience 'Which was the better son?' and was greatly surprised when they replied with one accord: 'The one who was polite to his father.' But Jesus, we are told, phrased the question somewhat differently and asked 'which of the two did what his father wanted?' – and to that there could be only one answer. Even so, Jesus spelt out the application (introduced by his authoritative 'Amen, I say to you') and told them:

> the tax collectors and prostitutes are entering the Kingdom of God ahead of you. For John came to you to show you the way of righteousness, and you did not believe him, but the tax collectors and prostitutes did. And even after you saw this, you did not repent and believe him.

When John preached, they were untouched; and when John called them to repentance, they saw no need for it. Once more, it was 'like John, like Jesus' – but with the responsibility for their heedlessness and refusal vastly increased.

The second parable in this trilogy is that of the Wicked Tenants (Matt. 21:33-43; cf. Mark 12:1-12; Luke 20:9-19). This parable faithfully 'reflects the social background of Jewish Galilee in the first century, with its great landed estates and the inevitable tension between the absentee-owners and the dispossessed, land-hungry peasantry who cultivated the land as tenant-farmers' (Lane, *Mark*, p. 416). Nor does the fact that the initial details were clearly derived from the Song of the Vineyard in Isaiah 5:1-7 detract from the realism of the story; but it does, perhaps, prepare us for the allegorical features which are inescapable in this parable.

Thus the slaves whom the owner sent first, according to custom, to collect his share of the crops clearly represent the Old Testament prophets,[13] many of whom were ill-treated and some even killed. It would be natural enough for it to occur to the presumably distant landowner that his son would have more authority, and command greater respect, than any slave emissaries – although we may well wonder, with Cranfield (*Mark*, p. 366), whether he would have ventured to send him to such violent and rebellious men without taking adequate precautions for his safety. But the tenant-farmers seem to have concluded that the owner had died, that his son was his only heir, and that if they killed him they might themselves claim the vineyard as 'ownerless property' (cf. Jeremias, *Parables*, pp. 75f.; I. H. Marshall, *Luke*, p. 730). So the sequel is scarcely surprising; for what owner (who was, in fact, far from dead) would not have done all he could to ensure that these wicked tenants should suffer a condign punishment and be replaced by men who would fulfil their obligations?

It seems clear in the parable (in which there was, I believe, a major 'allegorical' element from the beginning) that it was the premeditated murder of the owner's only son which precipitated his decisive intervention. So I believe with Cranfield that Jesus told the story to stir the consciences of those who were plotting his death (*Mark*, p. 367). We do not know whether the Jewish leaders detected the messianic claim which was implicit in the parable; but they can scarcely have missed its relevance to what they were planning. All three synoptic Gospels make it clear, moreover, that they realised that Jesus was predicting judgment on them and their nation, although only Matthew records the explicit words: 'Therefore I tell you that the Kingdom of God will be taken away from you and given to a people who will produce its fruit' – a saying which echoes the statement in Matthew 8:11 that 'many will come from the east and the west, and will take their places at the feast with Abraham, Isaac and Jacob in the Kingdom of heaven. But the subjects of the Kingdom will be thrown outside'. All the Synoptists, again, include at this point Jesus' quotation from Psalm 118:22f. about the stone that the builders rejected which eventually, in God's over-ruling providence, became the corner-stone; and both Matthew and Luke add the solemn warning; 'He who falls on this stone will be broken in pieces, but he on whom it falls will be crushed.'

The third of these parables is that of the Wedding Banquet (Matt. 22:1ff.). This is often taken as a 'doublet' to that of the Dinner Party in Luke 14:15ff.; but the differences are almost as obvious as the similarities, and it is common practice for an itinerant preacher to use an illustration with the same basic structure, but considerable variation of details, on more than one occasion. Matthew's story concerns the banquet that a king gave for the wedding of his son, and recounts how, when the guests who were originally invited spurned his repeated summons, the king sent his servants to extend the invitation to all and sundry.

It has often been observed that verses 6 and 7 (which state that some of the invited guests, not content with excuses for refusing the invitation, seized the king's servants, 'ill treated them and killed them'; and that the enraged king then 'sent his army and destroyed those murderers and burned their city') do not seem congruent with the rest of the story. So the suggestion has been made that a comment, written in the margin of a very early copy of this Gospel and based on the previous parable (21:35f.), became embodied in the text. But if this wedding banquet was the occasion for recognising the king's son as heir, the refusal of the summons and maltreatment of the messengers would have been tantamount to rebellion – and it is distinctly possible that any link with the previous parable was made by Jesus himself.

It is also often stated that verses 11-14, about the man who entered the feast without 'wedding clothes' and was subsequently thrown out, is in fact a separate parable. The hypothesis that a king, on such occasions, sometimes supplied his guests with robes from the royal wardrobe, seems to have dubious authority; and the question is asked how a last-minute invitee could be expected to be properly dressed. Yet all the others apparently were! The suggestion that these verses might be based on a different parable might find some support in the first verse of this chapter, where we are told that 'Jesus spoke to them again in parables' (in the plural). But the fact that we are told in verse 10 that the servants 'went out into the streets and gathered all the people they could find, both good and bad', together with the statement in verse 14 that 'many are invited, but few are chosen', make these verses far from irrelevant to this particular parable.

These hesitations about verses 6f. and 11ff. become largely irrelevant if we conclude that this particular parable, placed in this setting, was (even more than that of the Wicked Tenants) allegorical from the beginning. The invitation and repeated summons to the messianic banquet would then represent the preaching of the Gospel; the response of those originally invited (whether contemptuous disregard of the invitation or fierce hostility to the messengers) would depict the substantial rejection of that summons by the Jewish people; and the gathering in of people, 'good and bad', from the streets would point to the evangelisation of all and sundry. On this view the man who was ejected because he was improperly clothed would symbolise those who make some sort of response to the Gospel summons but whose trust is in their own efforts rather than divine grace, or whose commitment falls short of true regeneration.[14]

Two More Parables and a Quasi-Parable

Three more parables of the Kingdom (or two parables and one quasi-parable) are recorded in Matthew's Gospel – those of the Ten Virgins, the Talents and the Sheep and Goats (Matt. 25:1-46). The parables of the Ten Virgins and of the Talents (which is often regarded as a 'doublet' with that of the Pounds in Luke 19:11ff.) will be considered more fully in a subsequent chapter. They are, however, relevant to our present theme as illustrations of the fact that not all those who claim to be 'disciples', or who make an initial response to the good news of the Kingdom (a phenomenon which takes us back to the parable of the Sower), have genuinely accepted God's kingly rule. The salient feature in the parable of the Virgins, for example, is not that the 'foolish' ones 'became drowsy and fell asleep', for the wise did this too, but that they were wholly unprepared for the fact that the bridegroom would be 'a long time in coming'. In terms of today they may well typify nominal Christians, but the bridegroom's categorical statement: 'I tell you the truth, I don't know you', could never have been addressed to true disciples. They cannot have received that gift of new, divine life (which guarantees the grace of 'perseverance') that alone qualifies for entrance into the Kingdom.

Something broadly similar is also true, I think, of the parable of the Talents. Here the major ethical lesson is, no doubt, the obligation on all disciples to 'work out their own salvation with fear and trembling' and to be active in God's service – together with the fact that sins of omission are as serious as those of commission. But in our present context it is relevant to observe that a true disciple could scarcely say: 'Master, I know that you are a hard man, harvesting where you have not sown and gathering where you have not scattered seed' – and, indeed, that an intellectual faith which does not show itself in action is no 'saving faith' at all.

As already noted, the passage about 'the Sheep and the Goats' should not be taken as a parable in the conventional sense. In Tasker's words (*Matthew*, p. 237), it 'is a poetic description of the way in which the prophecy of Jesus in [Matthew] 16:27 will be fulfilled': that is, 'the Son of Man shall come in his Father's glory with his angels, and then he will reward each person according to what he has done'. Similarly, in this passage (vv. 31ff.), the Son of Man in his Parousia is both King and Judge, and the phrase 'all nations will be gathered before him' clearly refers to a universal judgment of individuals rather than a judgment of nations as such.

The parabolic feature in the account is provided by the familiar simile, in that milieu, of a shepherd separating his sheep from his goats – normally because the sheep could withstand the cold of a night in the open, while the goats had to be huddled together. But the salient feature in the application of this metaphor is the basis on which the 'sheep', who were given the place of acceptance and honour on the King's right hand, were distinguished from the 'goats', who were relegated to his left hand. The basic criterion was the attitude of each to the King himself, as demonstrated in what they had done, or not done, for 'one of the least of these brothers of mine'; and both 'the righteous' and 'those on his left' seem to have been equally amazed at his identification of himself with his 'brothers'. So the question inevitably arises how the phrase 'these brothers of mine' is to be understood.

There are, I think, three ways in which these words have been interpreted. Extreme 'Dispensationalists' have understood them to refer to the Jews, and make the criterion the way in which different nations have treated them. But this view seems to me virtually untenable. A much more plausible interpretation is to identify the 'brothers' with all human beings in any sort of need, on the basis that Jesus, we are specifically told, was 'made like his brothers in every way' (Heb. 2:17). On this view the 'righteous' are those who have, as Tasker puts it, made their election sure, not by constantly saying 'Lord, Lord', nor by repeated verbal expressions of their faith, but by numerous acts of self-sacrificing service, rendered unobtrusively to their fellow men (*Matthew*, p. 238).

The interpretation that I find most convincing, however, is that the phrase refers, primarily at least, to those who have themselves accepted, and seek to share with others, the kingly rule of God. Evidence for this view may be found in the fact that it was to his disciples that Jesus pointed when he said: 'Here are my mother and my brothers. For whoever does the will of my Father in heaven is my brother and sister and mother' (Matt. 12:49f.) Similarly, it was to the apostles that he said: 'If anyone will not welcome you or listen to your words, shake the dust off your feet when you leave that home or town. I tell you, it will be more tolerable for Sodom and Gomorrah on the day of judgment than for that town' (Matt. 10:14) – as a corollary of the fact that 'to receive you is to receive me' (Matt. 10:40). And it was to Saul of Tarsus, travelling to Damascus to persecute the infant Church, that the risen Lord said: 'Saul, Saul, why do you persecute *me*? (Acts 9:5).

Further support for this view can be found in the statement of Jesus to his disciples recorded in Mark 9:41: 'Amen, I say to you, anyone who gives you a cup of water because you belong to Christ will certainly not lose his reward.' On this Lane aptly comments:

> This statement presupposes ... that the *emissary of a man is as the man himself*, and what is done to the emissary is done to the one who sent him. Jesus thus recognizes that the cup of water is extended to himself, and that this act of kindness is actually a token of faith and obedience. That is why he solemnly promises that the one who declares himself 'for us' by this tangible action will not lose his reward. He will have a place in the Kingdom of God with the disciples and with Jesus, with whom he has identified himself in this small way. The reference to 'reward' carries no thought of deserving or of merit, for there is no way in which a cup of water may be conceived as *meriting* participation in the Kingdom (*Mark*, p. 344).

If this is so, then in this case, too, an understanding of this quasi-parable ultimately 'depends upon the recognition of Jesus as the Messiah and upon the recognition of the Kingdom of God which is breaking forth in his ministry' (p. 41 above). When men and women are truly confronted with the mission and message of Jesus, whether in his own person or when it is faithfully and effectively communicated by his followers, their eternal destiny depends on whether they accept him or reject him.

This may throw light on the somewhat mysterious answer that Jesus is recorded in Luke 17:20f. as giving to the Pharisees' question about when the Kingdom of God would come. 'The Kingdom of God does not come visibly', Jesus replied, 'nor will people say "Here it is", or "There it is", because the Kingdom of God is "among you" [or "within your grasp"].' If the translation 'within' is preferred, the meaning must be that the kingly rule of God is not manifested in this age in visible, apocalyptic sovereignty, but rather in the hearts of individual subjects; but if, as I believe, the translation 'among you' or 'within your grasp' is more appropriate to the context, then the reference is to the fact that the Kingdom of God had already come to his generation in the person of Jesus. But while his sovereignty was then veiled rather than 'visible', and has remained so until now, he was emphatic that one day men would in fact 'see the Son of Man coming with power and great glory' (Luke 21:27).

Thus in these later 'parables of judgment' we come back to the mystery of the Kingdom – already present in the Jesus of history, but still to come in its final consummation (cf. pp. 189ff. below). For, as Oscar Cullmann has put it:

The final act of the drama of the history of salvation cannot be neglected without disparaging the previous acts. If the death and resurrection of Christ are not to be consummated in the future, they cease to be the central event in the past, and the present is no longer located in the space between the starting-point and the consummation of Christology, ('Return', p. 160).

Chapter
3

The Kingdom of God, Eternal Life and Salvation

The Challenge of the Kingdom

In the last chapter we saw that the proclamation by Jesus of the Kingdom of God represents the very core and essence of his message and mission. We saw, too, that he devoted the majority of his matchless parables either to the 'mystery' of the Kingdom (as already present in his person, but still awaiting its consummation and visible manifestation at his Parousia),[1] or to the basis on which men and women can enter the Kingdom here and now, by their whole-hearted acceptance of God's kingly rule as their positive response to the challenge of Jesus, or they may eventually find themselves excluded from the eschatological Kingdom, to their bitter dismay, by reason of their negative or superficial response to that challenge. But Jesus had much more to say about the Kingdom than we have yet been able to mention even in passing, and he also used a number of other terms or figures of speech to express what is essentially the same teaching.

First, let us look back on the parables to which we have already referred. Many of them, as will have been noted, were based on the natural phenomena of a pastoral or agricultural economy (sheep and goats, sowing and reaping, seed and soil, wheat and weeds), while others were drawn from the familiar features of human life (domestic, social, economic, mercantile or political). This is why the parables of Jesus appealed so directly to the imagination of his hearers. Even the most ignorant and superficial must have found themselves readily involved in the situations he described. Their surface meaning was immediately apparent; and those whose primary concern was the satisfaction of their physical needs, or the desire to see some marvel performed, would probe no further. But these stories were very easy to remember, and the more thoughtful among his audience must often have pondered their deeper significance.

As we have seen, many scholars insist that the interpretation of the parable of the Sower represents the allegorising tendencies of the apostolic Church and cannot be regarded as the authentic teaching of Jesus himself. But this view seems to rest on very dubious foundations – chief among them an over-rigid distinction between a parable and an allegory (cf. pp. 39f. above). The argument that 'a story with a hidden meaning must be either a parable or an allegory', that 'we must so define the terms as to render them mutually exclusive', that 'Jesus told parables, not allegories', and that for this reason any story in the Gospels 'which falls within our definition of allegory . . . cannot be authentic', has been shown by G. B. Caird to contain a logical fallacy 'at every single step' (*Language*, p. 160f.). The vital point is to perceive what the author himself intended, rather than impose an artificial 'allegorisation' on his story, for

> there is a world of difference between allegorisation and an allegory. An allegory is a story intended by the author to convey a hidden meaning, and it is correctly interpreted when that hidden meaning is perceived. To allegorise is to impose on a story hidden meanings which the original author neither intended nor envisaged; it is to treat as allegory that which was not intended as allegory . . . If Jesus in fact composed similitudes with more than one point of comparison, it makes little difference to our understanding of them whether we call them parables or allegories, so long as we recognise that to identify intended points is not to allegorise (*Language*, p. 165).

That is excellently said; but it is a pity that Caird almost immediately remarks that 'a parable that needs to be explained is about as effective as an explained joke'. As has often been observed, the fallacy of thinking that a story with the most obvious moral message needs neither explanation nor application is decisively shown by David's reaction to Nathan's parable about the man with one ewe lamb. This story aroused David's instantaneous anger but apparently left his conscience wholly unruffled until the prophet said: 'You are the man'; and to conclude that the parable of the Sower, which needed to be explained as well as applied, was for that reason ineffective would be absurd. So I can see nothing improbable in the record that the disciples asked for, and Jesus gave, an explanation of some of his parables as a key to the rest (Mark 4:13).

Jesus also taught the same lessons both by the miracles he performed and by what may be termed 'enacted parables'. The most obvious example of the latter is, I think, the 'cursing' of the unproductive fig tree (Mark 11:12–14, 20:21 and parallels), but it is also clear that children sometimes provided Jesus with a 'visual aid' to illustrate some relevant truth about the Kingdom. To take children first, Matthew tells us that on one occasion Jesus answered the disciples' question 'Who is greatest in the kingdom of heaven?' by calling a child, getting him to stand among them, and saying: 'Amen, I say to you, unless you are converted [or 'changed'] and become like little children, you will never enter the kingdom of heaven. Therefore, whoever humbles himself like this child is the greatest in the kingdom of heaven' (Matt. 18:1–4).

A little later Matthew records that Jesus welcomed 'little children' with the words 'the kingdom of heaven belongs to such as these' (Matt. 19:13f.) On this Tasker comments that

Jesus is not saying here that children are outstanding examples of humility, or of any other virtue. He is pointing out that arrogant men and women can only possess the humility necessary for entrance into the kingdom of heaven if they are prepared to be insignificant, as little children were in the ancient world (*Matthew*, p. 175).

But I cannot myself believe that the comparison with a child is exclusively objective, for surely Jesus also intended to teach that the only way into the Kingdom is to be humble enough to accept it as a gift, in the way in which a child does not hesitate to take anything proffered by someone he trusts.

The incident of the fig tree is more difficult. Manson goes so far as to state that the Marcan narrative 'is a tale of miraculous power wasted in the service of ill-temper (for the supernatural energy employed to blast the unfortunate tree might have been more usefully expended in forcing a crop of figs out of season).' So he concludes that 'as it stands' this story is 'simply incredible'.[2] But if the incident is understood as an enacted parable to illustrate, on an insentient object, the judgment that inevitably awaited Jerusalem – and which ultimately awaits all those whose outward show of religion is devoid of any real 'fruit' – such a conclusion seems wholly out of place.

It is possible, of course, to argue that *some* fruit, however premature and unripe, usually appeared on a fig tree before the leaves, and *could* be eaten; so a tree in full leaf 'had all the appearance of being able to satisfy his hunger' (Tasker, *Matthew*, p. 201). But it seems better to conclude, with Cranfield, that

> Jesus may have used his hunger as an occasion for instructing his disciples. That is not to say that he expected to find edible figs . . . But that Jesus should look for fruit on a tree at a season when there was no chance of there being any is exactly the sort of thing we should expect, if this was a parabolic action; for an element of the unexpected and incongruous, which would stimulate curiosity, was a characteristic feature of the symbolic actions of the O.T. prophets (e.g. Jer. 13:1ff.; 19:1ff.) ... A people which honoured God with their lips but whose heart was all the time far from him (Mark 7:6) was like a tree with abundance of leaves but no fruit (*Mark*, pp. 356f.).

It is perhaps significant that in Mark's narrative references to the unproductive fig tree come immediately before and after the account of Jesus' cleansing of the temple – which can itself be regarded, from one point of view, as an enacted parable.

This book is devoted to the teaching of Jesus, so any adequate consideration of his miracles lies beyond its scope. But it is clear that in all the Gospels his 'mighty works' (whether in exorcism, healing, raising the dead or nature miracles) are recorded as demonstrations of his authority in deed as well as word (Mark 1:22, 27) and as signs that in his advent the Kingdom of God had indeed come (Matt. 12:28). His exorcisms were a foreshadowing of the fact that, when the Kingdom is consummated, the power of evil will be finally broken (cf. Luke 11:20); his healing miracles of the perfect health (or full salvation) of body as well as spirit that will then prevail; his resuscitation of the dead of the new life he has come to give here and now – a life that will be enhanced, rather than diminished, by physical death; and his nature miracles of the eschatological Kingdom in which he will 'make all things new'. In his own words his miracles were wrought by God's Spirit or 'finger' (Matt. 12:28; Luke 11:20), demonstrating that he was the 'Anointed One' whose coming was foretold in Isaiah 61 (Luke 4:16-21); they provided visible evidence that the 'Son of Man' had authority on earth to forgive sins (Mark 2:3-12); and they gave expression not only to his own compassion but to the mercy of God the Father (Luke 6:36).

One of the more difficult problems is 'the binding of Satan' as symbolised in the exorcism of demons. We have already seen how Jesus is reported by Matthew as saying: 'If I drive out demons by the Spirit of God, then the Kingdom of God has come upon you'; and he went on to ask his disciples how anyone can 'enter a strong man's house and carry off his possessions unless he first ties up the strong man?' (Matt. 12:28f.). To exorcise demons, as well as preach and heal the sick, was part of the commission he gave to the Twelve when he sent them out (Mark 6:7); and Luke tells us that, when the seventy (or seventy-two) returned from a very similar mission,[3] they joyfully told him: 'Lord, even the demons are subject to us in your name'. To this Jesus is recorded as replying, 'I saw Satan fall like lightning from heaven', and to have said that he had, indeed, given them authority to act in his name, but that instead of rejoicing that the spirits were subject to them, they should rejoice that their names were 'written in heaven' (Luke 10:18ff.).

On this, a number of brief comments must, I think, be made. First, there can be no doubt that the victory of Christ over the powers of darkness is a central feature of the Gospels. We must, of course, be very careful not to confuse mental or psychiatric disorder with 'demon possession', which requires exorcism rather than medical treatment, and to remember that on one occasion Jesus described a crippled woman he had healed as having been 'kept prisoner by Satan' (Luke 13:16), but it is clear that in places the New Testament records point to a basically spiritual phenomenon – sometimes seen today, it seems, in those who have dabbled in the occult. Cranfield has pertinently remarked that 'the spread of a confident certainty of the demons' non-existence' may well have represented their greatest triumph (*Mark*, p. 75).

Secondly, the statement 'I saw Satan fall like lightning from heaven' is almost certainly to be understood as a metaphor in the sense of the logion in John 12:31: 'Now is the time for judgment on this world; now the prince of this world will be driven out' – a statement immediately followed by a reference to the victory of the Cross. But that victory (cf. Col. 2:14f.), foreshadowed in the earthly ministry of Jesus and the authority he delegated to his disciples, will be consummated and openly manifested only at the Parousia. That is why he bade his disciples to rejoice primarily in the sure prospect that they would share in the ultimate triumph of the Kingdom, rather than its present foretaste (cf. Green, *Downfall, passim*).

Another problem is posed by the apparent contradiction between the words recorded in Mark 9:38-40, on the one hand, and in Matthew 7:21-3, on the other. In the first passage Jesus tells his disciples not to try to restrain the activity of an unknown exorcist, who was 'driving out demons' in his name, because he was not one of their company, and adds 'Whoever is not against us is for us'. In the second, by contrast, he solemnly warns them that 'Many will say to me on that day, "Lord, Lord, did we not prophesy in your name, and in your name drive out demons and perform many miracles?" Then I will tell them

plainly "I never knew you. Away from me, you evildoers".'
The explanation of this seeming contradiction presumably lies in the fact that the exorcist to whom the disciples took exception was using the name of Jesus in sincerity and faith, unlike the unbelieving exorcists about whom we read in Acts 19:13ff.; so Jesus bade his disciples not to be narrow and sectarian, but to welcome any true disciple. In Matthew 7:21ff., on the other hand, he insisted that it was not those who made an outward show of religion who would enter the Kingdom, but only the man 'who does the will of my Father who is in heaven'. Somewhat similarly, Tasker's comment on the categorical statement in Matthew 12:30 that 'he who is not with me is against me' is that

the long-expected reign of God has now arrived, though not yet in its fullness. Satan is already bound though not so as to be rendered completely impotent (vv. 28, 29). Nevertheless, the campaign between God and Satan has begun in earnest, and in that campaign neutrality is impossible. Not to be allied with Jesus and the kingdom of God is to be allied with Satan and the kingdom of evil; and to try to prevent men and women from accepting Jesus as their King, as the Pharisees were trying to do (vv. 23, 24), is to disintegrate and *scatter* those who would otherwise be 'the sons of the kingdom' (*Matthew*, p.128).

Eternal Life

But although the concept of the Kingdom of God was central to the teaching of Jesus, he also used a number of other comparable terms – such as 'salvation' and 'eternal life'. These two concepts seem indeed to have been regarded as almost synonymous with the Kingdom. An outstanding illustration of this is provided by the story of 'The Rich Young Man' recorded in Mark 10:17-26, with its parallels in Matthew 19:16-26 and Luke 18:18-29. In each case the question he asked was what he must do 'to inherit eternal life';[4] but this incident provoked a discussion between Jesus and his disciples about who can 'enter the kingdom of God', and the disciples asking him 'who then can be saved?'

There can be no doubt that in Jewish thought 'eternal life' meant life 'in the coming age' which (in the language of the New Testament) man 'inherits', 'receives', 'gains' or 'enters into' (Vincent Taylor, *Mark*, p. 426). Precisely the same idea was inherent in the Jewish concept of the eschatological Kingdom and messianic salvation, so there is no wonder that in this story the three terms are almost interchangeable. But in the teaching of Jesus the Kingdom, eternal life and salvation were already present in his person, and men could enter into an experience of God's kingly rule, of new life and of his saving power here and now, although the consummation of this three-fold concept was still to come.

The teaching in this story about riches must be reserved for a subsequent chapter. What is relevant in this context is that eternal life, the Kingdom and salvation cannot be 'earned' by trying to keep the Old Testament commandments (which the young man had clearly done to the best of his understanding and ability), but only by a whole-hearted personal commitment to Jesus himself. There is considerable controversy about why Jesus replied to the man's original question (in the Marcan and Lukan versions of the story) by asking 'Why do you call me good? No one is good – except God alone.' All Jews would, of course, have agreed that only God is *absolutely* good; so the question is whether Jesus repudiated this epithet as inapplicable to himself – and, if so, in what sense.

One perfectly feasible explanation is that Jesus was drawing his questioner's attention to the true meaning of the phrase he had used, and what it should properly imply, without any repudiation of the title. But if Jesus' reply made 'a tacit contrast between the absolute goodness of God and his own goodness as subject to growth and trial in the circumstances of the Incarnation' (Vincent Taylor, *Mark*, p. 427), we need to remember that Jesus repeatedly emphasised his complete dependence on the Father. So here he 'directs the young man's attention away from himself to his Father, who is the only source and only norm of goodness' (Cranfield, *Mark,* pp. 327f.). The relevance of this to the young man's question (how he might inherit eternal life) was that Jesus' immediate reply pointed to the fact that it was from God alone that such life proceeds, while his subsequent call to 'follow me' gave a clear indication of where, and how, that life could be found.

It is in the Fourth Gospel that we find the most extensive teaching about life which is new, abundant and eternal. As early as chapter 3 the fact that this is virtually a synonym for the Kingdom – in the double sense of a present experience of the kingly rule of God and future entrance into his eschatological Kingdom – is made perfectly clear in Jesus' statement to Nicodemus: 'Amen, amen I tell you, unless a man is born again [the Greek may mean either 'a second time' or 'from above'], he cannot see the kingdom of God' (v. 3). These words are expanded in verse 5, when (with the same emphatic introduction) Jesus told him that 'unless a man is born of water and the Spirit, he cannot enter the kingdom of God'. To Nicodemus the word 'water' could only have pointed to John the Baptist's call for repentance in preparation for the Kingdom, and Jesus explained what birth of the 'Spirit' meant when he said: 'Just as Moses lifted up the serpent in the wilderness, so the Son of Man must be lifted up, that everyone who believes in him may have eternal life' (vv. 14f.).

The intimate connection we have already noted between eternal life and 'salvation' is spelt out in the next two verses, where Jesus goes on to say: 'For God so loved the world that he gave his only begotten Son, that whoever believes in him shall not perish but have eternal life. For God did not send his Son into the world to condemn the world, but to save the world through him'. On these verses R.L. Lightfoot aptly comments that

> God's purpose ... is declared to have been solely positive, not negative; salvation, not condemnation (cf. Rom. 8:32-4). On the other hand, since the Son of God, Himself love, life, light and truth, has come into the world, and there is no love, life, light, or truth which does not take its origin from Him

[1:3], acceptance of His witness and consequent devotion to Him are essential [8:31, 15:22, 16:9]; and rejection of Him or disbelief in Him is therefore acceptance of and identification with hatred, death, darkness and falsehood [8:44, 47, 15:23] (*John*, p. 118).

And the way in which the person, mission and message of Jesus inevitably act as a catalyst is reiterated at the end of the chapter in the words: 'Whoever believes in the Son has eternal life, but whoever rejects the Son will not see life, for God's wrath remains on him'.[5]

In the next chapter, in his conversation with the Samaritan woman, Jesus adapts his metaphor to the situation and speaks of 'living water'. When asked if he was greater than Jacob, who had dug the well at which they were conversing, Jesus replies: 'Everyone who drinks this water will be thirsty again, but whoever drinks the water that I shall give him will never suffer thirst any more. The water that I shall give him will be an inner spring always welling up for eternal life' (John 4:13ff.).

On this John Marsh comments that 'Jesus would draw a contrast between the *water* of the Torah (the Torah was often likened to water), which provided a law 'external' to men, and his own *water* of the Spirit, which was internal to men, an interior guide'. Then, in a more detailed note, he adds:

> The contrast between drink that can only quench the thirst for a short time, and then needs to be repeated and the drink which, drunk once only, quenches all further thirst, reminds the reader of the contrast in Hebrews between the sacrifices of the old order which had to be repeated daily, and that one sacrifice of the new order which, once offered, is universally and everlastingly efficacious. The point made is the same (*John*, pp. 212 ff.).

More immediately, Jesus' words here remind us of his invitation on the last day of the Feast of Tabernacles: 'If anyone is thirsty, let him come to me; whoever believes in me, let him drink. As Scripture says, "Streams of living water will flow from within him."' And the Evangelist adds: 'By this he meant the Spirit, whom those who believed in him were later to receive' (John 7:37f.).

Much of the ensuing conversation was largely unintelligible to the woman; but it was enough to arouse her messianic expectations. So Lightfoot comments:

> She is still unable to discern in the Traveller the Word become flesh, the Son of man; but she is able to express her conviction that One will come and, having come, will make all things clear; and this enables the Lord to direct her forthwith to the Object of her hope. He, of whom she has spoken, is even now present, and is talking with her (*John* p. 124).

Previously, as his habit was, he had spoken to her about the Father; and when his disciples came and urged him to eat he could say 'My food is to do the will of him who sent me and to finish his work.' And this in turn led him to speak to them about sowing and reaping in terms that equated the harvest with 'eternal life', in which 'sower and reaper may rejoice together' (John 4:34ff.). The final harvest was, of course, still future; but there was also an immediate reaping, for we read that 'Many Samaritans of that town came to believe in him because of the woman's testimony', while 'many more became believers because of what they heard from his own lips'. 'We know', they said, 'that this man really is the Saviour of the world' (John 4:39-42).

In chapters 5 and 6 teaching about eternal life, as both a present possession and a future prospect, comes again and again. The discourse (John 5:19-47) which immediately follows the healing of the crippled man lying beside the pool of Bethesda was primarily devoted to the relationship of the Son with the Father, in obedience to whom and dependence on whom he both lived and taught. This will concern us later (cf. p. 156). But it is noteworthy in our present context that in 5:24f. Jesus is reported as saying: 'Amen, amen, I say to you, anyone who gives heed to what I say and puts his trust in him who sent me has eternal life, and will not come up for judgment, but has already passed from death to life. Amen, amen, I say to you, a time is coming, indeed it is already here, when the dead shall hear the voice of the Son of God, and all who hear shall come to life'.

Of these verses R.L. Lightfoot aptly observes: 'Since this life is declared to be a possibility, indeed a fact, of the present, it is unnecessary to refer to physical death; the death mentioned in 5:24 is the state out of which a man has passed when he hears and obeys the word of the Lord, in other words, believes in Him' (*John*, pp. 143f.). But almost immediately Jesus went on to say that 'the time is coming when all who are in the grave shall hear his voice and come forth; those who have done right will rise to life; those who have done wrong will rise to hear their doom' (vv. 18f.) – where the reference is clearly to the Day of Judgment. Later in the same chapter, he emphasised that eternal life was something he alone could give, for he told his hearers: 'You study the scriptures diligently, supposing that in having them you have eternal life; yet, although their testimony points to me, you refuse to come to me for that life' (vv. 39f.).

In chapter 6 he makes this even more explicit when he tells them that they 'must work', not for the 'perishable food' with which the five thousand had been fed, 'but for the food that lasts, the food of eternal life'. When they ask him what they must do if they are to work as God would have them work, he makes the categorical statement: 'This is the work that God requires: believe in the one whom he has sent' (vv. 27ff.). He then goes on to declare: 'I am the bread of life. He who comes to me will never go hungry, and he who believes in me will never be thirsty' (v. 35). This clearly points to a present experience here on earth. When, however, he states in verse 40 that 'it is my Father's will that everyone who looks to the Son and puts his faith in him shall have eternal life; and I will raise him up on the last day', he was equally clearly referring to the life beyond.

Later in the chapter he explains the metaphorical statement 'I am the bread of life' by saying that 'the bread which I will give is my own flesh; I give it for the life of the world'. In other words, the eternal life he gives derives from his broken body and atoning death. There is no other way; for he tells them, in words which must have been particularly shocking to a Jewish audience (to which the consumption even of animal blood was explicitly forbidden), that 'unless you eat the flesh of the Son of Man and drink his blood you can have no life in you. Whoever eats my flesh and drinks my blood possesses eternal life, and I will raise him up on the last day' (vv. 53f.). But, whatever the shock, his hearers can scarcely have thought that he was advocating cannibalism, even when he continued: 'My flesh is real food and my blood is real drink' (v. 55).

Obviously enough, the words are figurative, as William Temple insists. 'There is no magical sacrament to be appointed any more than there is a reversion to primitive savagery. "The Spirit is the Life-giver" as we confess in the Nicene Creed: "the flesh" – even the flesh of the Son of Man, literally understood – "doth not profit at all; the words that I have spoken to you are spirit and life" (v. 63).' Why then, Temple asks, did not Jesus say 'Spirit and Life' from the first, and thus have avoided 'very great complexity' and a 'hard saying' which alienated many? To this he replies:

> To talk about receiving a Spirit or even Life is ineffective as a challenge. It easily coheres with a vague religiosity which has no definite and critical moments, no fixed religious practice, no cutting edge ... It is vital for our spiritual well-being that we be brought to the point of specific worship, wherein we seek to receive Christ into our souls. But we must not only receive Him in some general way, or by recollection of such scenes from his life as we prefer to contemplate. We must receive Him in the fulness of His self-sacrifice ... The Gospel finds its focus, not in the happy scenes of Galilee, but in the Cross and Resurrection. It is the Body broken and the Blood outpoured that we must receive as our own life (*Readings*, p.98).

It is scarcely possible for a Christian to read this passage without thinking of the Last Supper and its symbolism. But John has – deliberately, no doubt – attached this discourse on

the Christian's need to feed on the atoning death of his Lord to
the miracle of the Feeding of the Five Thousand rather than
to the institution of the Eucharist, which is not specifically
mentioned in this Gospel. In Temple's words, John

> will not have the Sacrament isolated either from God's
> general activity in the world or from the fulness of Christian
> life. The 'Real Presence' in the Eucharist is a fact, but it is not
> unique. The Word of God is everywhere present and active
> ... So soon as the Sacrament is isolated it becomes in greater
> or less degree magical (*Readings*, pp.81f.).

We participate in his life whenever we listen to his words, as
Peter made clear when this discourse caused many disciples to
withdraw and Jesus asked the Twelve whether they, too,
wanted to leave him. 'Lord, to whom shall we go?' Peter
replied. 'You have the words of eternal life' (v. 68).

In chapter 10 Jesus returns to the subject of the gift of
eternal life based on his atoning death, this time by means of the
metaphor of sheepfold, sheep and shepherd. 'I am the door', he
declared; 'anyone who comes into the fold through me shall be
safe. He shall go in and out and shall find pasturage' (v.9). This
was the very purpose for which he had come: 'that men may
have life, and may have it in all its fullness' (v. 10). So he was
not only the door, but the shepherd – the 'Good Shepherd' who
'lays down his life for the sheep', 'knows' them, and seeks to
'bring in' others who do not yet belong to 'this fold' (vv. 11,
14ff.). The relationship between shepherd and sheep is
reciprocal. On their part, 'my own sheep listen to my voice; I
know them, and they follow me' (v. 27). On his part, he not only
gives them 'eternal life' but guarantees their final salvation; for
'My Father who has given them to me is greater than all, and no
one can snatch them out of my Father's hand' (vv. 27ff.). And
in the next chapter Jesus again spells out the two tenses of this
'eternal life' when he says to Martha: 'I am the resurrection and
I am life. If a man has faith in me, even though he die, he shall
come to life; and no one who is alive and has faith in me shall
ever die. Do you believe this?' (11:25f.) The secret is that to

'know God' as he is revealed in Jesus *is* eternal life (17:3).

Salvation

Salvation is an ever recurring theme throughout the Old Testament, both as a present experience and an eschatological prospect. Time and again, prophets and psalmists raise a paean of praise to the God who not only provides salvation by delivering his people from enemies or calamities, but has himself 'become their salvation' (cf. Exod. 15:2). Yet, mingled with this gratitude and joy, we find a deep longing for a deliverance which still seemed far away (cf. Isa. 59:11), but would ultimately be manifested to the ends of the earth (Isa. 52:10). And in the New Testament, as we have seen, salvation is so closely linked with the Kingdom of God and with eternal life in the teaching of Jesus that the three concepts are virtually synonymous.

In the Infancy Narratives Mary rejoices in 'God my Saviour' (Luke 1:47); Joseph is told to give the name Jesus (Saviour) to the son to whom Mary is to give birth (Matt. 1:21); and Zechariah praises the God of Israel because 'he has turned to his people, saved them and set them free' (Luke 1:16ff.). But the only context in which Jesus himself is recorded in the Gospels as using the noun 'salvation' is in his encounter with Zacchaeus the tax collector (Luke 19:1-10). After Jesus had invited himself to his house, Zacchaeus declared: 'Here and now, sir, I give half my possessions to the poor; and if I have cheated anyone, I am ready to repay him four times over'. To this Jesus replied with the words: 'Salvation has come to this house today! – for this man too is a son of Abraham, and the Son of Man has come to seek and save what is lost'.

In this context 'salvation' presumably does not refer to Jesus himself, who had literally come to that house, but to the transformation that his visit had effected in Zacchaeus. The phrase 'for this man too is a son of Abraham' is taken by some commentators [6] to mean that Zacchaeus had shown himself to be one of Abraham's spiritual progeny by his response to this encounter; but Howard Marshall is probably right in arguing that the term *kathoti* 'is used to introduce an antecedent reason rather than a subsequent proof' (*Luke*, p. 698), so the point of the saying may be that a Jew, even though he has become one of the 'lost sheep of the house of Israel', is one of those to whom Jesus was specifically 'sent' (Matt. 15:24). But the same use of *kathoti* would also cover Caird's suggestion that a man like Zacchaeus would never have exposed himself to the hostility of a large crowd unless he had either been prompted by a burdened conscience or attracted by the welcome Jesus was known to give to social outcasts (*Luke*, pp. 207f.).

In the New Testament, then, the primary meaning of salvation is eschatological: salvation from sin, judgment and the 'wrath' of God. But the words 'save' and 'saved' are repeatedly used also for deliverance from death, disease, demon possession, bondage to evil or any sort of calamity. So salvation, even in the spiritual and eschatological sense of the term, is not exclusively future, but – like eternal life and a personal experience of the kingly rule of God – something that begins here on earth. This is implicit in Jesus' declaration that 'The Son of Man has come to seek and save what is lost', and explicit in the parables in Luke 15 of the lost Sheep, the lost Coin and the lost Son, all of which are recorded as his reply to the complaint of the Pharisees and doctors of the law that 'this fellow welcomes sinners and eats with them'.

It is true that these parables may be said to indicate three – or, rather, four – different ways of being 'lost': by straying, little by little, like a sheep in search of pasture; unconsciously, like an insentient coin; by deliberate choice, like the 'prodigal son'; or in self-complacency, like the elder brother. But the basic emphasis is common to all three parables: the joy experienced by one who recovers what he has lost; and we are explicitly told that this joy is only a pale reflection of the way in which God rejoices over 'one sinner who repents' (vv. 7 and 10). Almost inevitably, perhaps, the Christian is apt to read these three stories against the mental background of the 'Good Shepherd', who even gave his life for the sheep; the Spirit, who quickens the insentient; and the 'Prodigal Father', who welcomes his wayward son without a word of reproach and longs for his self-satisfied elder brother to join in the rejoicing. But this is an apt example of 'allegorising' three parables which all point to the God who, far from being an impassible, philosophical abstraction, 'loved the world so much that he gave his only Son, that everyone who has faith in him may not perish, but have eternal life' (John 3:16).

The reciprocal joy of the one who is 'found', 'saved' and knows that he 'has already passed from death to life' (John 5:24) is vividly depicted in the parables of the Treasure and the costly Pearl. As we have observed (p. 44 above), the statement that the man who found each of them 'sold everything he had and bought it' (the field in which the treasure lay hidden, or the pearl itself) is parabolic language, for the New Testament is emphatic that eternal salvation can never be earned or purchased. It is the gift of God, the cost of which is borne by him alone, and must be accepted with the ingenuous simplicity of a child (Mark 10:15).

But it must be remembered that Jesus' initial proclamation, as recorded by Mark, was that 'The time has come; the Kingdom of God is upon you; repent, and believe the Gospel'. In other words, the reception of the good news of the free gift of salvation must be accompanied by repentance, or a radical change of mind. Instead of continuing in a state of alienation from the kingly rule of God (in sin, on the one hand, or the pursuit of self justification, on the other), the one who is confronted with the Kingdom in the person of Jesus must whole-heartedly submit to his claims. But this is emphatically not another way of saying that man must, after all, merit his salvation; for the New Testament makes it clear that repentance itself is the gift of God, granted to those who humbly ask for it.[7]

This submission to Jesus as Saviour and Lord represents the 'narrow gate' that 'leads to life', which opens out, in its turn, to the road of discipleship. This, too, is described as 'narrow' (Matt. 7:13f.): not, surely, in the sense of being narrow-minded, legalistically rigid or restricted in interests or sympathies, but in that of the self-discipline of a soldier on active service, with a war on his hands – against 'the world, the flesh and the devil'. To take these in the reverse order, the Christian has a powerful enemy without, a traitor within and a hostile environment around him. He will be put to the test and tempted by the one who tested, and tried to seduce, his Master (cf. Luke 22:31); he will find that his fallen nature acts very much like a fifth columnist who sides with the enemy (cf. Mark 9:43-7); and he will experience opposition from fellow human beings and the social system they create (Matt. 5:10ff.).

In other words, the Christian life is no 'easy option'; and the divine promise is that 'the man who holds out to the end will be saved (Mark 13:13): that is, vindicated by God and delivered from terrestrial warfare and suffering. This may seem a bleak prospect but, as in the case of 'repentance', we are not left to our own resources. Our 'treasure' or future inheritance is safe from either despoliation or decay (Matt. 6:19f.); Jesus has promised to be with us to the very end (Matt. 28:20); and although we shall be 'hated', and *may* even be put to death, we have been assured that 'not a hair of your head shall be lost', in the ultimate sense (Luke 21:16f.)[8]

What this adds up to is that Satan – as the embodiment of temptation and evil – is a very real and powerful adversary, as both the teaching and experience of Jesus himself, of the apostles, and of Christians down the ages amply prove. There is also no room for doubt about the fact that the Christian must 'persevere' or 'hold out' to the end (Matt. 24:13). Jesus himself stated without equivocation: 'I tell you this: everyone who acknowledges me before men, the Son of Man will acknowledge before the angels of God' (Luke 12:8f.). I think it is fair to conclude that the reference here is to an open confession – and a public, deliberate and possibly even forensic denial. Even so, the story of Peter's denial (which was public, if not forensic) proves that the one who 'disowns' Christ, even in the most emphatic terms (Mark 14:66-72), can be forgiven and restored – as the statement in Luke 12:10 about the 'unforgivable sin' makes abundantly clear. It is true that belief in the final 'perseverance' of all those who are true disciples raises a number of theological problems, and that many are convinced that even a sincere Christian may apostasise; but I believe the teaching of the New Testament as a whole suggests that, while it is sadly possible for a true Christian to 'backslide', and while the parable of the Sower makes it clear that an initial response to the message of the Gospel may not represent real regeneration, one who is regenerate can never finally be 'snatched' out of his heavenly Father's hand (John 10:29).

The 'flesh' and the 'world' require somewhat less comment. By regeneration the Christian receives a new – even a 'divine' – nature (John 3:6; cf. 2 Peter 1:4); but this does not mean that his former, fallen nature is totally removed (cf. Mark 9:43-7). That will happen only at the Parousia, or when he sees Christ in his glory (John 17:24; cf. 1 John 3:2). As for the 'world', this term is used in the recorded teaching of Jesus in a number of different senses. At times it simply means the earth, its human inhabitants, this present age, or terrestrial life.[9] Elsewhere it refers to those anxieties, temptations and pressures that assail a Christian as a result of living in the environment of a world which, although still owing its true allegiance to the God who made it, is at present largely under 'enemy occupation' (cf. John 12:31; 14:30; 16:11).[10]

As a result, Satan succeeds in preventing large numbers of people from so much as hearing the message of the Kingdom, salvation and eternal life in such a way as to make any positive response – as the fate of the seed sown on the footpath indicates (Mark 4:4). But he does more than this, for he assiduously sows weeds or darnel among the wheat (cf. p. 44 above); and, just as the 'wheat' in the parable of the Weeds stands for 'the children of the Kingdom', the darnel represents 'the children of the evil one' (Matt. 13:38) – or, in other words, the citizens of a very different 'kingdom' (Mark 3:24ff.). This is why Jesus warned his followers that 'All men will hate you because of your allegiance to me' (Mark 13:13), and that this allegiance would even split families apart (Luke 21:51ff.). In this world, he said, the 'wheat' and the 'darnel' would 'grow together'; but, just as the one is divided from the other at the time of harvest,

so at the end of time the Son of Man will send out his angels,

who will gather out of his kingdom everything that causes
offence, and all those whose deeds are evil, and these will be
thrown into the blazing furnace, the place of wailing and
grinding of teeth (Matt. 13:40ff.).

Warnings even more terrible than this – which speak of outer
darkness, unquenchable fire, grinding of teeth, and even of a
devouring worm which never dies – recur in all the synoptic
Gospels.[11] As noted below (pp. 89f., 91f.), some of these metaphors were derived from Isaiah 66:24 and were later applied to
the Valley of Ben Hinnom (Gehenna), which became a symbol
of judgment (Jer. 7:31ff.; 19:6f.) which was regularly used, during
the inter-testamental period, for the eschatological fire of hell.
The metaphorical language in which these awesome warnings
are couched must not be taken literally (for outer darkness and
unquenchable fire scarcely cohere); but it should certainly not
be 'explained away' (Cranfield, *Mark*, p. 314).
    The basic element in all the passages concerned is that they
point to a condemnation and destruction which are final and
irreversible, sometimes described as 'the second death' (Rev.
2:11, 20:14; 21:8). But Luke 12:47f. seems to indicate that
divine justice will be able in some way to adjust judgment to
responsibility – as, indeed, reward to fidelity (Luke 19:12-26).
It has been aptly noted that the 'absolute division' in the quasi-
parable of the Sheep and the Goats (Matt. 25:31-46) is 'between
inheriting "the Kingdom prepared for you from the foundation
of the world" (v. 34) and going "into the eternal fire prepared
for the devil and his angels" (v. 41; not for men). "Eternal
punishment" and "eternal life" (v. 46) are not necessarily the
same in duration. "Eternal" (Gk. *aiōnios*) simply refers to the
age to come and makes the point that the division is final for
men's destiny' (Nixon, 'Matthew', p. 846).
    To sum up, in the message and mission of Jesus the promised
Kingdom of God was not only heralded but actually
inaugurated. He offered eternal life as a gift to anyone who
would turn to him in faith from the sin that is common to us all
and from the attempts to earn salvation that seem to be
endemic in those who take 'religion' seriously. He taught that it

was the despised tax collector, who threw himself on the mercy of God, rather than the pious, upright but self-satisfied Pharisee, who went home 'acquitted' or 'justified' (Luke 18:9-14), and that our love for the one who forgives is proportionate to our consciousness of how much he has forgiven us (Luke 7:36-50). Thus his message was one of free, unmerited forgiveness to *any* repentant sinner, without qualification – to be followed by exceedingly exacting standards for discipleship (cf. pp. 102f. below). This is in striking contrast to the practice of social clubs today, which rigorously scrutinise candidates for election, but are usually very tolerant about their subsequent behaviour!

There are certain passages in the teaching of Jesus on which the common assertion that he himself believed that his Parousia was imminent can be based: but other passages point strongly in the opposite direction. We shall return to this controversial subject in chapter 8. For the meantime he gave the most explicit assurances of the Father's ceaseless care for his adopted children, to which he called them to respond with their complete confidence, saying

> How little faith you have! And so you are not to set your mind on food and drink; you are not to worry. For ... you have a Father who knows that you need them. No, set your mind on his kingdom, and all the rest will come to you as well. Have no fear, little flock; for your Father has chosen you to give you the Kingdom (Luke 12:29-32).

Here he was referring, of course, to the eschatological Kingdom, in which 'Abraham, Isaac and Jacob, and all the prophets' – to say nothing of all those who in Old Testament days turned to him in repentance and faith – would share (Luke 13:28). He also insisted that in this life, too, 'even the least in the Kingdom of heaven' is more privileged, and richer in potential experience, than John the Baptist, pre-eminent though he was (Matt. 11:11); whereas on the day of judgment those who had rejected his proclamation of the Good News, and his call to repentance, would be in a much worse position than those of

Tyre, Sidon or Sodom (Matt. 11:20-4). It was not only possessions that his disciples must be willing to give up, but family ties and even life itself. But the reward in the eschatological Kingdom would be correspondingly great: the best of all, to hear his 'Well done, good and trusty servant! Come and share in your Master's delight' (Matt. 25:21ff.).

Part II

The Ethics of
the Kingdom

Chapter
4

The Law, the Prophets and the Kingdom

There can be no doubt that we must begin our study of the ethical teaching of Jesus with an assessment of the relationship between his mission and message and the Mosaic Law – or, for that matter, the Old Testament revelation as a whole. Jesus certainly did not start his own work and teaching from a vacuum. On the contrary, he had pondered the Law and the Prophets long, deeply and radically. He gave full recognition to their divine authority and was at considerable pains to make a sharp distinction between them and the rabbinical accretions, and even subtractions, which had become attached to them. He did not simply confirm the continued authority even of the Old Testament revelation itself, for he saw clearly that both Law and Prophets had been pointing forward to him, to the New Covenant he was to inaugurate and to the Kingdom he himself personified and would one day bring to consummation. So we must note throughout this chapter the balance, which could so easily have been a tension, between what was recognised as originally authoritative but shown to be transient, on the one hand, and his own words which would never pass away, on the other.

The *locus classicus* for the teaching of Jesus about the relationship between his own mission and message and the Old Testament is undoubtedly Matt. 5:17-20, as illustrated in the six antitheses which immediately follow (vv. 21-48). These verses are, indeed, almost as controversial as they are crucial, for they raise a number of difficult problems regarding their precise interpretation, mutual coherence and basic compatibility with other passages in the Gospels. It is not surprising, therefore, that scholars have put forward a plethora of suggestions: that these verses emanate from a Jewish-Christian milieu rather than from Jesus himself; that some four separate sayings have been brought together in a sequence which is far from homogeneous; and that the passage as a whole cannot be reconciled either with its component parts or with the teaching of the rest of the New Testament (unless, indeed, we import certain qualifications which do not arise naturally from – or, in some cases, seem clearly inappropriate to – the wording as it stands). Many of these points will necessarily concern us as we consider the passage clause by clause; but some of the more radical critical suggestions, which I do not myself find at all convincing, lie outside the scope of this chapter.

The Basic Passage (Matt. 5:17-20)

The words 'Do not suppose that I have come to abolish the Law or the Prophets; I have not come to abolish them but to fulfil them' (v.17) do not seem to me to present any great difficulty, although they have been the subject of much controversy. The opening phrase 'Do not suppose . . .' occurs again in Matthew 10:34, and *may* point to some explicit misunderstanding (occasioned, perhaps, by an incident like the controversy between Jesus and the Pharisees about Sabbath observance recorded in Mark 2:23-8) that Jesus wished to dispel or elucidate. However this may be, the words represent a natural introduction, whether original or redactional, to teaching on a subject which clearly stood in need of elucidation: the relationship of Jesus to the Old Testament – for that, almost certainly, is the meaning of 'the Law or the Prophets' in this context.

The Hebrew Bible – as we now have it, at least – is made up of three divisions: the Pentateuch (designated 'Moses' or 'the Law', in the narrowest sense of that term); the Prophets; and the Writings (in which the book of the Psalms held pride of place, as the reference to it in Luke 24:44 indicates). But in the New Testament 'the Law' is itself said in Matthew 11:13 to 'prophesy'; and the term is at times used in reference to the Old Testament as a whole. Thus the first half of this verse represents a decisive statement that Jesus, in both proclaiming and inaugurating the Kingdom of God (cf. Matt. 4:17; 5:19 and 20; etc.), had not come to destroy or 'abolish' the Old Testament Scriptures – for the Greek word *kataluō* is primarily used of demolishing or tearing down buildings, and then, as here, of abrogating or destroying something of a less material substance. Far from 'scrapping' either the Law or the Prophets, then, Jesus affirmed that he had come to 'fulfil' them.

But what precisely does this word (*plēroō*) mean in this context? Some scholars, both Jewish and Christian, gloss the word as meaning that Jesus came to establish or confirm the Mosaic law.[1] This is certainly not the sense in which his disciples, or the Early Church, understood this verse, as is obvious from the fact that they soon came to see that his teaching about inward and outward defilement, as recorded in Mark 7:14-23, made the dietary laws of the Old Testament obsolete; and it cannot have been long before they realised that his supreme sacrifice of himself on the Cross 'once for all' had made any further animal sacrifices meaningless and theologically repugnant. It is only by making a sharp distinction between what has been termed the 'moral law', on the one hand, and both the 'ceremonial' and 'civil' (or 'judicial') law, on the other (in company, for example, with the Thirty-Nine Articles of the Church of England and with a number of Puritan divines), that this meaning of *plēroō* could possibly be sustained in this context. And although I myself believe that this classification of the Mosaic law serves to help us, in retrospect, to distinguish the very different ways in which Jesus may be said to have 'fulfilled' its heterogeneous strands, it would have been largely incomprehensible to Israel of old, is certainly not explicit in the New Testament and is decisively excluded, in this context at least, by the next two verses.

Many Christian commentators,[2] on the other hand, suggest that Jesus 'fulfilled' or 'completed' the Law and the Prophets simply by extending their scope, their meaning and their moral demands. This is certainly true of the teaching he gave about some of the Old Testament commandments, but it cannot properly be applied to either the Law or the Prophets in their entirety; for it is clear that some of the requirements of the Mosaic law were in fact superseded, rather than extended, by the mission and message of Jesus. It is in this context that Robert Banks argues persuasively that

> precisely the same meaning should be given to the term *plēroun* when it is used of the Law as that which it has when it is used of the Prophets. The prophetic teachings point forward (principally) to the actions of Christ and have been realised in them in an incomparably greater way. The Mosaic laws point forward (principally) to the teachings of Christ and have also been realised in them in a more profound manner. The word 'fulfil' in 5:17, then, includes not only an element of discontinuity (that which has now been realised *transcends* the Law) but an element of continuity as well (that which transcends the Law is nevertheless something to which the Law itself *pointed forward* (Banks, *Law,* p. 210).

So the antithesis in this verse is not between 'scrap' and 'retain', in the sense of 'preserve just as they were', but between 'abolish' and 'fulfil', in the sense 'give them the particular fulfilment that was always intended, and is in each case appropriate'. This is why D.A. Carson, when commenting on this verse in the light of the series of more detailed antitheses in the rest of the chapter, justly remarks that 'In no case does this "abolish" the Old Testament canon, any more than the obsolescence of the levitical sacrificial system decimates the canon' (*Matthew, ad loc.*)[3].

Jesus introduces the next verse with his characteristic and authoritative 'Amen, I say to you,' and then continues: 'until heaven and earth disappear, not the smallest letter, not the least stroke of a pen, will by any means disappear from the Law until everything is accomplished'. Here 'the Law' almost certainly stands for the Old Testament as a whole, and unquestionably accords it the highest authority; but Carson justly remarks that verses 18 and 19 do not, strictly speaking, 'wrestle with the authority of the Old Testament in the abstract, but with the nature, extent and duration of its normative validity'. The *nature* of that validity has already been indicated – certainly by implication – in the previous verse, while its *extent* is underlined by the categorical reference to 'one jot or one tittle'; but an equal emphasis, in this verse, falls on the question of the *duration* of the authority of these detailed Old Testament pronouncements, as prescribed by the two 'until' clauses. The first of these clearly represents the equivalent of 'until the present age comes to an end', while the second presumably means that not one detail will fail to have its appropriate fulfilment in the person, teaching and work of Jesus (Carson, *Matthew, ad loc.*).

The Greek word here translated 'accomplished' is frequently used in Matthew of 'something which happens in fulfilment of prophecy', and the sense of this verse 'may well be that in this age nothing shall pass away from the Old Testament until everything which it predicts about the Messiah has happened and so been given its full significance' (Nixon, *Matthew*, p. 823). Thus, while the Law has not been abrogated, 'it is in the demands of the Kingdom, not in its own continued existence, that the Law is validated' (Banks, *Law*, p. 222). It is significant that all three Synoptists record that, on another occasion, Jesus declared that 'Heaven and earth will pass away; but my words will not pass away' (Matt 24:35; Mark 13:31; Luke 21:33).

The most difficult problem in these controversial verses, as I see it, is the precise meaning of the reference in verse 19 to 'these commandments', the least of which must be both obeyed and taught to others (rather than 'set aside, as the Qumran community accused the Pharisees of doing) by all those who aspire to have a place in the eschatological Kingdom of God. It is tempting again to follow Robert Banks, in his major study *Jesus and the Law in the Synoptic Tradition* (pp. 222f.), in interpreting 'these commandments' as referring to Jesus' own teaching, in line with the instruction in the Great Commission not only to 'make disciples of all nations', but to teach them 'to obey everything I have commanded you' (Matt. 28:19f.). I cannot myself, however, believe that this interpretation of the Greek word *entolai* fits either the present context or the somewhat parallel passage in Luke 16:16f., where the statement 'The Law and the Prophets were proclaimed until John. Since that time, the good news of the Kingdom of God is being preached, and everyone is forcing his way into it' is immediately followed by the significant addendum: 'It is easier for heaven and earth to disappear than for the least stroke of a pen to drop out of the Law'. To suggest that either of these passages can be adequately construed as meaning that all the specific commandments in the Old Testament as a whole, or the Pentateuch in particular, have been superseded – without trace or remainder – by the teaching of Jesus seems to me virtually untenable.

Yet neither can the reference to 'the least of these commandments' be taken to mean the least of the Mosaic commandments as they were promulgated. As we have already seen, what we may for convenience term the 'ceremonial' law was made obsolete by both the teaching and redemptive work of Jesus, and it is clear that the 'judicial' law, promulgated for the practical governance of an ethnic nation, could no longer have literal reference when the Kingdom of God has been 'taken away' from the Jews and 'given to a people who will produce its fruit' (Matt. 21:43). This 'people' would be drawn from 'every nation, tribe, people and language' (Rev. 7:9), each of which would have their own civil and criminal law; and on them it is the basic moral law (as revealed in the Old Testament and expounded in the New) which is incumbent – for that law, which gives expression to the character of the Lawgiver, is as unchangeable as God himself. But this threefold classification of the Mosaic law is a theological deduction which can scarcely be called in aid in the exposition of these verses.

So I incline to the view that the term 'these commandments' here refers primarily to those of the Old Testament in general, without this rule of thumb classification. What verse 19 would seem to mean, then, is that not one of these commandments is to be 'scrapped' or disparaged, since every one of them played its part in pointing forward to the teaching and mission of Jesus (cf. Carson, *Matthew, ad loc.*). He 'fulfilled' them all, but in a variety of different ways. Some he simply reinforced; some, again, he extended in scope or reinterpreted in content by spelling out the direction in which they were designed to point; and yet others found their final fulfilment in his unique work of redemption. It is always by reference to his teaching and mission, therefore, that we should keep and teach them today.

This interpretation is, I think, reinforced by verse 20, where Jesus emphatically states that 'unless your righteousness surpasses that of the Pharisees and the teachers of the law, you will certainly not enter the kingdom of heaven'. In the context of putting into practice and, even more, of teaching the 'least' of the Mosaic commandments, the Pharisees and the teachers of the law could, in the main, scarcely be faulted. So when Jesus insisted that the righteousness required from those who would enter the Kingdom of God is higher (not lower) than theirs, he must have been referring not to quantity so much as quality, not to outward so much as inward obedience, not to the Old Testament Scriptures as fulfilled only in his teaching, but also in his redemptive work. This is why Matthew sums up the series of specific antitheses in vv. 21-47 by the comprehensive – and in itself totally impossible – command: 'Be perfect, therefore, as your heavenly Father is perfect' (Matt. 5:48).

As emphasised elsewhere in this book, the ethical teaching of Jesus is that of the Kingdom or reign of God, so it is not surprising that it is couched in absolute terms. It represents the 'pure, unconditioned will of God without compromise of any sort'. It is in this light that we must interpret this demand for God-like 'perfection'. Viewed from one angle, as G. E. Ladd aptly remarks, Jesus' ethics are quite unattainable.

If the Sermon on the Mount is legislation to determine admission into the future Kingdom, then all men are excluded ... Jesus required perfect love, a love as perfect as God's love for men. If Jesus demanded only legalistic obedience to his teaching, then he left men hanging over the precipice of despair with no word of salvation ... This righteousness, as Dibelius has said, can be perfectly experienced only in the eschatological Kingdom of God. It can nevertheless to a real degree be attained in the present age, insofar as the reign of God is actually experienced ... Even as the Kingdom has invaded the evil age to bring to men in advance a partial but real experience of the blessings of the eschatological Kingdom, so is the righteousness of the Kingdom attainable, in part if not in perfection, in the present order. Ethics, like the Kingdom itself, stand in the tension between present realisation and future eschatological perfection (Ladd, *Presence*, pp. 291f.).

This is precisely where the New Covenant, which Jesus told his disciples he was going to inaugurate by his atoning death (Mark 14:24), comes in – for this constitutes an outstanding example of the way in which Jesus came not 'to abolish the Law or the Prophets ... but to fulfil them'. To take this Covenant in its reverse order, it was to be founded on a full and free pardon which includes justification (which is in Greek a word cognate with the 'righteousness' demanded here); to consist in an experimental, personal knowledge of God; and to entail a 'writing' of his law in his peoples' minds and hearts – so that they begin to think and desire to live accordingly.

Six Illustrative Antitheses

The six specific examples of an antithesis between what Jesus' hearers had 'heard that it was said to the people long ago' and the authoritative teaching of Jesus himself seem to confirm this interpretation. David Daube regards the thesis, in each case, as corresponding to the rabbinic 'I might understand literally', and the antitheseis to the rabbinic 'But thou must say' – the latter based either on another text from Scripture or a logical deduction. In rabbinic usage, however, this represents 'academic, dialectic exegesis', with the reason for the preferred view clearly stated; whereas in these verses we have before us, not a scholarly working out by some Rabbis of a progressive interpretation as against a conceivable narrow one, but a laying down by Jesus, supreme authority, of the proper demand ... The setting in life of the Rabbinic form is a dialectic exposition of the Law; that of the Matthean is proclamation of the true Law (Daube, *Rabbinic Judaism*, pp. 57ff.).[4]

These six illustrations are by no means homogeneous, and have been classified by commentators in a number of different ways. There is wide disagreement, for example, not only about which of them should be regarded as 'original' as distinct from 'redactional', but also which of them reinforce, extend or transcend the Mosaic law and which must be held, in some sense at least, to supersede it. The fact is that in each case Jesus contrasts the way in which the law was previously understood or misunderstood with the true direction in which it pointed, as determined by his own authority as its 'fulfiller'.

The first example, in verses 21-6, is concerned with hatred and anger. Here the thesis consists of the prohibition of murder in the Decalogue (Exod. 20:13), together with a summary of the Old Testament attitude to anyone who commits this offence, while the antithesis takes the form of three radical statements in which Jesus declares that anger, insult and contempt must also stand condemned in the context of the 'better' righteousness which is demanded in the Kingdom (v. 22), and that anyone who has caused someone else to react in this way must immediately seek reconciliation (vv. 23-6). In other words, the sixth commandment not only forbids murder as such but points forward to the total exclusion of hatred or the incitement of hatred (from one of which, of course, murder commonly springs) in the eschatological Kingdom. So Jesus demands that this spirit should prevail, here and now, among those who have accepted God's sovereignty and reign.

It has often been remarked that the Gospels record that Jesus was himself 'moved with anger' on a number of occasions, which seems at first sight inconsistent with this teaching. But this apparently categorical condemnation of anger was never understood to apply to what has been termed 'righteous anger' – as the words 'angry with his brother *without cause* (which are found in several manuscripts in this context), and the explicit exhortation in Ephesians 4:25 ('If you are angry, do not let anger lead you to sin; do not let the sunset find you still nursing it; leave no loop-hole for the devil') clearly indicate.

Jesus was himself conspicuously gentle, forbearing and forgiving in any matter which concerned him personally, but he could and did speak in devastating denunciation of religious hypocrisy, the exploitation of others or leading children into sin. Although he made it clear that in the Incarnation he had come not to judge the world but to save it (John 3:17), he combined in his person both the Suffering Servant and the destined Judge of all men (John 5:22), for the eschatological Kingdom will be consummated not only in salvation but in judgment. Human anger almost always includes a personal, petty or vindictive element. It is only in God himself (and Jesus as God-in-manhood) that love for the sinner goes hand in hand with hatred for the sin which spoils his life and cuts him off from divine fellowship – coupled with an offer of free forgiveness which can be humbly accepted or defiantly, even thoughtlessly, spurned.

In the second example, in verses 27–30, Jesus turns to the question of lust. The thesis here is a straightforward citation of the seventh commandment in the Decalogue (Exod. 20:14). To say that, in the antithesis, Jesus was *'equating* the covert desire with the overt act'[5] or, as I have often heard people assert, that he taught that lust 'is *just* as sinful as adultery', is manifest nonsense. To begin with, it is clearly less sinful to toy with tempation, or even surrender to it in part, than to give way to it completely. But the major difference between lustful thoughts and actually committing adultery is that, in the latter case, the woman concerned is involved in the sin (and the woman's husband, at least, in the injury this causes), while in the former case the sin is confined to the individual – unless, of course, the suggestion is right that the wording of verse 28 in Greek really means 'so as to get her to lust' (that is, for a man so to look at a woman as to provoke lust in her and thus entice her to sin) (Carson, *Matthew*, *ad loc.*).

Verses 29 and 30 are far from otiose, since references to 'eye' and 'hand' were, it seems, often made in rabbinical warnings against adultery. The eye is here regarded as the medium through which temptation comes, and the hand (and elsewhere the foot) as symbolising a physical response. The injunctions to 'gouge it out' and 'cut it off' are, of course, metaphorical, for Jesus not infrequently used hyperbole in his teaching. To give such phrases a literal and physical meaning – as, for example, in the voluntary castration sometimes practised in both the early and medieval Church – is to misunderstand them. Their true meaning is that 'a limited but morally healthy life is better than a wider life which is morally depraved.' That is true Christian asceticism. If certain books, places, activities or company are causes of temptation, 'they must be eschewed whatever the cost' (Tasker, *Matthew*, p. 69).

What is crystal clear, in this antithesis, is that Jesus was not 'abrogating', in any sense of that term, the seventh commandment, but bringing out its moral import and implications in a much more radical way than the traditional rabbinic teaching. In regard to the reference to 'the fire of hell' in verse 22, and to 'bodies' being 'thrown' (or 'going') into it in verses 29 and 30, J. S. Whale aptly comments:

I know it is no longer fashionable to talk about hell, one good reason for this being that to make religion into a prudential insurance policy is to degrade it. The Faith is not a fire-escape. But in rejecting the old mythology of eternity as grotesque and even immoral, many people make the mistake of rejecting the truth it illustrated (which is rather like rejecting a book as untrue because the pictures in it are bad) (Whale, *Doctrine*, p. 186).

The 'old mythology' concerned was largely derived from an over-literal understanding of some of the references to hell in the New Testament, which are based on the imagery in Isaiah 66:24 about dead bodies 'whose worm will not die, nor will their fire be quenched'. The word used for hell in the New Testament is usually Gehenna, which represents the Hebrew for 'the valley of the son of Hinnom'. It was here that human sacrifices were offered by fire to Molech, and it became a symbol of all that was abominable (cf. pp. 74, 191f.).

The third example, in verses 31 and 32, concerns divorce. Here the thesis is not based on the Decalogue, but on the regulations in Deuteronomy 24:1–4, which were designed to provide suitable safeguards against unfettered divorce, although in the antithesis Jesus clearly emphasised the link that exists between divorce and the seventh commandment. The teaching in these two verses is expanded in Matthew 19:3–11; and parallels, with certain differences, are recorded in Mark 10:2–11 and Luke 16:18. The theme, in each case, is the Creator's intention that marriage should constitute a life-long union of man and wife in mutual fidelity; but Jesus is not depicted as questioning the divine authority of the Mosaic concession to the 'hardness' of men's hearts.

We must discuss the difficult subject of divorce in more detail in the chapter devoted to 'Social Ethics' (cf. pp. 130ff. below). What is relevant at this point is to take note of the fact that Jesus here goes far beyond the text of Deuteronomy 24:1–4, to say nothing of rabbinic teaching, in spelling out the moral implications of a further marriage into which the husband may embark, or a wife (particularly in those days) almost be forced, after a wrongful divorce. This is commonly claimed as an example of Jesus' abrogating the Deuteronomic regulations rather than declaring their 'true intention' (cf. Banks, *Law*, p. 193). But it would be more accurate to say that he 'fulfilled' the Law by insisting that the direction in which it pointed was the sanctity and permanence of marriage, and then carried this principle much further. I am, however, by no means certain that these two verses, as expanded in Matthew 19:3–11 and in the other synoptic Gospels, should be regarded as a dominical prohibition, to which there can be no possible exception, to remarriage after a divorce in any circumstances at all – or in any circumstances other than unchastity (cf. pp. 132ff. below). 'This is the absolute ethic of the Kingdom', as R. E.

Nixon has justly insisted, 'which is no more meant to be a subject for legislation than anything else in the passage' (Nixon, 'Matthew', p. 823).

The subject of the fourth example, in verses 33-7, is oaths. Here the thesis is 'not a precise quotation but an accurate summary of Old Testament teaching on the subject' (Tasker, *Matthew*, p. 66), in which the commandments in the Decalogue not to 'misuse the name of the Lord' or to 'give false testimony'[6] had been extended to an obligation to keep oaths that had been sworn and vows that had been taken.[7] In the antithesis Jesus not only exposed the hollowness of rabbinical casuistry in holding that an oath which did not actually profane the name of Yahweh need not necessarily be kept (Matt. 5:34 ff.; 23:16-22), but insisted that a simple statement, whether in the affirmative or negative, should be sufficient in itself ('let your "Yes" be "Yes", and your "No", "No".') (Matt. 5:37).

By forbidding those oaths which were designed, in the Mosaic legislation, to ensure truth and guarantee honesty, but which were in fact often misused in the interests of falsehood and double-dealing, Jesus did not 'abolish' (i.e. 'destroy') the Law, but he undeniably substituted his own authoritative teaching which 'fulfilled' its basic purpose in a much more radical way. As Banks insists, the words 'Do not swear at all' (*holōs*) admit, as such, of no equivocation; but I think he misunderstands the manner of Jesus' teaching (especially as recorded in the 'Sermon') in apparently making no exception whatever – even in regard to a formal oath when this is required in a court of law. To this, it seems, Jesus himself submitted (Matt. 26:63f.); and it is clear that Paul did not hesitate to invoke God as his witness on occasions[8] – so the echo of Matthew 5:37 in James 5:12 should probably be interpreted, primarily at least, in the context of James' teaching about patience and warning against sins of speech (cf. James 5:7-12; 1:26).

The fifth example, in verses 38-42, focuses on the way in which a Christian should react to aggression. The thesis represents the *lex talionis*, as enunciated in Exodus 21:24,

Leviticus 24:20 and Deuteronomy 19:21. This was intended as a basis for judicial sanctions rather than personal revenge; and it represents the maximum that the injured person may demand. In the antithesis, however, Jesus exhorts his disciples not to react to an aggressor in any such way but rather, on the contrary, to be ready to sacrifice their own interests to those of others.

It is clear that Jesus deliberately used a measure of hyperbole in the illustrations given in these verses. When the Kingdom is consummated, all human aggression, litigation, government and need will alike be at an end; and those who have already accepted God's kingly rule and messianic salvation should give substance to this fact here and now in their human relationships. Revenge or retaliation for personal insult is unequivocally forbidden; but it is doubtful if the reference to coat and shirt in verse 40 should be taken literally, and I cannot myself believe that verse 41 means that there are *no* circumstances in which a tyrannical government may legitimately be resisted, or that verse 42 teaches that *every* request for help must be granted in the very terms in which it is made – for this is not the way in which our heavenly Father shows his incomparable love. However this may be, in this antithesis Jesus may be said, again, not to have 'abolished' the law of the Old Testament but to have transcended it by his own authoritative teaching.

The sixth example, in verses 43–8, concerns both love and hatred. Here the thesis consists of a quotation from Leviticus 19:18 (which in fact commands the people of Israel to 'love your neighbour *as yourself*') coupled with a summary of what some scribes evidently taught[9] (or the inference that was commonly drawn) in the addition 'and hate your enemy' – contrary although this clearly was to the teaching of Exodus 23:4f. Then, in the antithesis, Jesus goes beyond both what was 'written' in the Old Testament and 'said' to the people long ago (or, perhaps, to his own contemporaries) in his categorical command: 'Love your enemies and pray for those who persecute you'.

He also declares the motive for this exceedingly high

standard when he adds 'that you may be [that is, 'show yourselves to be'] sons of your Father in heaven', whose 'common grace' is bestowed on the evil as well as the good (v. 45). On these verses, Plummer aptly observes: 'To return evil for good is devilish; to return good for good is human; to return good for evil is divine' (*Matthew*, p. 89). In the parable of the Good Samaritan (Luke 10:25ff.), moreover, Jesus gave his own distinctive interpretation of the word 'neighbour'.

I have already commented on verse 48: 'Be perfect, therefore, as your heavenly Father is perfect', so I will merely remark that it is clear from this whole passage that Jesus regarded the Old Testament as instinct with divine authority. No instance is recorded in the Gospels in which he himself broke the Mosaic law – for he, as a Jew, had been 'born under the law' (Gal. 4:4) – although he often disregarded, and even denounced, the burdensome, nit-picking and sometimes basically mistaken rabbinic teaching which 'expounded' it. But, as the Messiah to whom the Old Testament had looked forward, he exercised his authority sometimes to draw out its deepest principles, sometimes to transcend or supersede them, and sometimes to declare the substance to which they had pointed like sign-posts.

Two Further Illustrations

I shall conclude this chapter with two more illustrations of Jesus' attitude to the Law, whether written or oral, in regard to questions about which much controversy is recorded in the Gospels: sabbath observance and ceremonial purity.

All three synoptic Gospels record the incident in which the Pharisees asked Jesus why his disciples were picking some heads of grain, rubbing them in their hands, and eating them on the Sabbath (Mark 2:23ff. and parallels). It is explicitly stated in Deuteronomy 23:25 that 'If you enter your neighbour's grainfield, you may pick kernels with your hands, but you must not put a sickle to his standing grain'; so no question of theft arose, and their behaviour would have been perfectly lawful on any other day. The rabbinic law, however, equated picking the kernels with reaping and rubbing them in their hands with threshing: that is, with doing 'work' – which was, of course, forbidden on the Sabbath (Ex. 20:8). But Jesus would have none of this, and reminded them of how David, with his companions, had once eaten the consecrated bread (1 Sam. 21:1ff.) which only the priests were permitted to eat (Lev. 24:5ff.).

The precise point of relevance of this story has been much debated. Matthew states that the disciples 'became hungry', while in commenting on Luke's account Earle Ellis suggests that the disciples' act was 'probably part of a meal during a preaching tour' (Ellis, *Luke*, p. 108) – so it has been inferred that the priority of human need, or the demands of 'mission', over ritual regulations provides the connecting point between the two incidents. Another theory is that what David did may well have been on a sabbath; but his act would have been unlawful on any day. Matthew tells us that Jesus also referred to the fact that the priests in the Temple 'desecrate' the Sabbath without incurring any blame; but this was specifically provided for in the written Law (Num. 27:9f.). There is, I think, only one basic solution, recorded in each of the synoptic Gospels; namely, that 'the Son of Man [greater than either David or the Temple] is Lord of the Sabbath'. Mark prefaces this claim with the words: 'The Sabbath was made for the sake of man not man for the Sabbath' (Mark 2:27). So, if David could break the ritual rules of the written Law – not in a spirit of blasphemous defiance (cf. Num. 15:30) but to meet human need – how much more could Jesus permit his disciples to ignore what was only a rabbinical interpretation of the written Law?

Both these principles (that is, the proper interpretation of the sabbath law in the economy of Israel as a sign of the covenant of Sinai, and the complete authority of Jesus in the new situation which his advent had brought about) can be seen at work in the healing miracles that Jesus performed on the Sabbath, to one of which each of the synoptic Gospels immediately turns (cf. Mark 3:1ff. and parallels). This was performed in a synagogue, and concerned a man with a 'shrivelled' hand. Those who were looking 'for a reason to accuse Jesus' were 'watching him closely', for the rabbinic law allowed medical aid on the Sabbath only in an acute case where the patient's life was in immediate danger. But this principle would not apply to a man with a shrivelled hand – or, indeed, to a crippled woman, a demon-possessed man, one afflicted with dropsy or paralysis, or one congenitally blind.[10]

In some of these cases Jesus rebuked his critics for their hypocrisy by pointing out that they themselves would, on the Sabbath, have rescued a donkey, ox or sheep (Luke 14:5; cf. Matt. 12:12),[11] and would regularly untie and water their domestic animals (Luke 13:15). We are told that he was both distressed and angered at their false scale of values and rigid scrupulosity (Mark 3:5); that the people at large were amazed by his authority (Mark 1:27; Luke 4:6), although their leaders were enraged (Mark 3:6; John 5:16; etc.); and that he laid down the general principle that, if 'the Sabbath was made for man', then it must be 'lawful to do good' on that day (Matt. 12:12). But the basic point is that in all these cases human need was met by messianic authority; and there can be no doubt that it was the claims that were implicit (at least) in that authority which were the chief cause of the Pharisees' fury. It is in this context that John writes:

> So, because Jesus was doing these things on the Sabbath, the Jews persecuted him. Jesus said to them, 'My Father is always at his work to this very day, and I, too, am working.' For this reason the Jews tried all the harder to kill him; not only was he breaking the Sabbath, but he was even calling God his own Father, making himself equal with God (John 5:16).

It was not the assertion that God was still 'working', even on the Sabbath, that upset them; for the Rabbis taught that, after God had ceased from his work of creation, he was 'still unceasingly active as Upholder and moral Governor or Judge of the world' (Lightfoot, *John*, p. 140). What enraged them was that he had called God 'his very own Father', in a way that seemed to them both blasphemous and rebellious – 'for in rabbinic teaching a rebellious son was described as "making himself equal" with his father; that is to say, he assumes charge of his own life as an independent person, and no longer recognises his father's authority' (Marsh, *John*, p. 257).

This is why Jesus 'answered and said', with a triple repetition (John 5:19, 24, 25) of his emphatic 'Amen, amen, I say unto you', that in fact his dependence on the Father was absolute. First, he told them what has been termed 'The Parable of the Son as Apprentice'; for C. H. Dodd has pointed out that verses 19 and 20a *could* be translated, in quite general terms, as 'a son can do nothing on his own; he does only what he sees his father doing: what father does, son does; for a father loves his son and shows him all his trade' (Dodd, *More Studies*, pp. 30ff.). But at this point this 'hidden parable' reveals itself as part of what R. L. Lightfoot describes as 'a defence of Christian monotheism', as Jesus expounds, first negatively and then positively, 'the complete union in action between the Father and Himself . . . due to the absolute dependence, in all things, of the Son upon the Father' (Lightfoot, *John*, p. 141). So if God 'worked' without cessation in doing good to his creatures, then Jesus must continue his messianic work of beneficence and proclamation on every day of the week. Thus, to return to the synoptic tradition, it was not only as the Messiah, son of David, or even as the representative and apocalyptic 'Son of Man', that Jesus could claim to be 'Lord of the Sabbath'. In the Old Testament the Sabbath was repeatedly described as 'a Sabbath to the Lord your God' (Ex. 20:10); so the implications of this claim were unmistakable.

My last illustration concerns the law regarding ritual 'uncleanness', whether in the Pentateuch itself or in the oral law of the Rabbis. It was in the context of rabbinic regulations about eating with 'unclean hands' – that is, without a ritual wash after coming in from the market – that Jesus gave some of his most radical teaching (Matt. 15:1ff.; Mark 7:1ff.).

When the Pharisees criticised some of his disciples for not following 'the tradition of the elders' in this respect, he turned on them and not only told them that Isaiah's statement about people who 'teach as doctrines the commandments of men' was relevant to them, but that in some cases they went so far as to 'neglect the commandment of God' in order 'to hold fast' to their own tradition (e.g. Mark – quoting Isa. 29:13). The specific example of this he is recorded as giving in this context was the 'Corban' procedure,[12] by which obedience to the command to 'honour your father and mother', in so far as its financial aspects were concerned, might be both evaded and actually made illicit. But he also, by his categorical statement that 'Nothing outside a man can make him "unclean" by going into him ... it is what comes out of a man that makes him "unclean" ', authoritatively substituted the principle of moral purity for the dietary laws of the Pentateuch (as was realised when Mark wrote his Gospel) – and, indeed, for the whole concept of ceremonial 'cleanness'. As Cranfield justly observes, this was an abrogation of ritual regulations by the one who was, and knew himself to be, 'the end of the law' (Rom. 10:4; Cranfield, *Mark*, p. 244). In place of ceremonial defilement he unequivocally put his emphasis on moral sins – 'evil thoughts, sexual immorality, theft, murder, adultery, greed, malice, deceit, lewdness, envy, slander, arrogance and folly' (Mark 7:21f.).

Emil Schürer has observed that in the Old Testament and, still more, in the practice and teaching of the Pharisees 'a separation from uncleanness is always a simultaneous separation from unclean persons' (*History,* II, p. 396). In the Old Testament this is applied to those suffering from various skin diseases or forms of bodily discharge, and to dead bodies. It is clear, however, that Jesus did not regard himself as being made ritually 'unclean' by taking the hand of a dead girl, by touching a 'leper' (probably to express love as well as convey healing), or by being touched by a woman with a hae-morrhage[13] – and he does not seem to have been criticised on this account (partly, perhaps, because of the healing power he conveyed). What he was bitterly criticised for was his contacts and 'table fellowship' with tax-collectors and 'sinners' (Matt. 9:6ff., etc.), for the Pharisees 'separated themselves not only from the homes and society of Gentiles and half-Jews, but from the uncleanness which, in their view, adhered to a great part of the Jewish nation' (Schürer, *History*, II, p. 396). This went far beyond the Mosaic law which, for all its insistence on rules concerning cleanness, 'never intimates that these are trans- gressed if one eats with another who has not observed these regulations' (Banks, *Law*, p. 11).

Jesus completely disregarded this rabbinic teaching. He did not shrink from being called 'a friend of tax collectors and "sinners"' (Matt. 11:19; Luke 7:34); he welcomed the devotion of a repentant prostitute (Luke 7:36ff.); and he told his critics to 'go and learn what this means: "I desire mercy, not sacrifice"' (Matt. 9:12f., quoting Hosea 6:6). It was not the well, but the sick, who needed a doctor; not those who regarded themselves as righteous, but those who knew that they were sinners, who needed a Saviour; and it was to them that his mission was primarily directed.

No wonder, then, that Jesus is recorded as insisting that any attempt simply to sew his message and mission like a patch on to the old fabric, or to pour them like wine into the old wine- skins, could only end in disaster. As Banks trenchantly puts it:

> The real issue that is constantly brought forward in his teaching is not so much that of his keeping or not keeping the Law, or of the relationship of his teaching to it. It is the failure of his opponents to realise that his presence has inaugurated a new situation with respect to the things of God, and that it is no longer the Law but his own teaching that is decisive (*Law*, p. 131).

It seems to me that the Transfiguration uniquely emphasises the two fundamental conclusions about Jesus and the Old Testament Scriptures for which I have been contending. On the one hand, the way in which both the Law and the Prophets pointed forward to Jesus – and, indeed, to his atoning death – is thrown into bold relief by the fact that Moses and Elijah appeared to the three apostles talking with Jesus 'about his "exodus", which he was about to bring to fulfilment at Jerusalem' (Luke 9:31). On the other hand, Peter's impulsive suggestion that they should erect three 'booths' or 'tents' for all three was decisively silenced by the heavenly voice which declared: 'This is my beloved Son: listen to him' (Mark 9:7). As Jesus himself put it, 'Until John, it was the Law and the Prophets: since then, there is the good news of the Kingdom of God ...' (Luke 16:16).

Chapter
5

The Personal Ethics of the Kingdom

In our last chapter we discussed the attitude of Jesus towards the teaching of the Old Testament, since it is obvious that it was on this that his own mission and message were founded. For this purpose we relied chiefly on The Sermon on the Mount – together with the very similar teaching recorded by Luke in what is commonly called 'The Sermon on the Plain'.[1] There can be no doubt, indeed, that Matthew 5–7 are among the most widely acclaimed passages in the New Testament. Many contemporary Jews would, for example, substantially agree with Joseph Klausner's statement that

> The main strength of Jesus lay in his ethical teaching. If we omitted the miracles and a few mystical sayings which tend to deify the Son of Man, and preserved only the moral precepts and parables, the Gospels would count as one of the most wonderful collections of ethical teaching in the world (*Jesus*, p. 381).

Later in the same book Klausner affirms that 'in his ethical code there is a sublimity, distinctiveness and originality in form unparalleled in any other Hebrew ethical code' (p. 414).

Now it is certainly right to emphasise the sublimity, distinctiveness and originality of Jesus' teaching, yet virtually impossible to isolate it from the works of love and power which so often prompted it or flowed directly from it. And it is still more impossible to think of this teaching in a vacuum apart from the person and claims of the one who gave it, or the spiritual impact it made on many of those who heard it. It is a grave mistake, for example, to regard the Sermon on the Mount as the New Testament equivalent to the Decalogue, and then to assert that if only men and women in every land would accept its ethical precepts, and attempt to put them into practice in their everyday lives, the world would not only be an infinitely better place to live in, but the Kingdom of God would be 'brought in'.

It is in the context of Klausner's statements quoted above that T. W. Manson pertinently remarks that it is

necessary to lay down at the outset that the 'Ethics of Jesus', in the sense in which Dr Klausner speaks of them and many others think of them, do not exist and never have existed. Nor will such a book ever exist save by the process of tearing some of the moral aphorisms of Jesus out of their true context and fitting them into another and probably alien context ... The notion that we can wander at will through the teaching of Jesus as though through a garden, plucking here and there an ethical flower to weave a chaplet for the adornment of our own philosophy of life, is an idea that is doomed to disappointment, for the nature of plucked flowers is to wither. The ethical maxims of Jesus, abstracted from the religion out of which they grow, become mere counsels of perfection which we may indeed respectfully admire, but which have no immediate reference to the affairs of our ordinary life (*Teaching*, pp. 285f.).

This simply means that Jesus in this respect stood in 'the direct line of succession to all the prophets and psalmists and sages of Israel', for 'the idea of ethics as an independent discipline' would have been alien to them all. To the Semitic mind (for this applies just as much to Islam as to Judaism) theology and ethics must of necessity go hand in hand, in theory if not always in practice. And when we turn to the Sermon on the Mount it is immediately obvious that this is no system of ethics designed for mankind in general – vastly though society would benefit from an attempt to put its principles into practice – but for the disciples of Jesus to whom it was originally given, and for all those subsequent disciples who accept the kingly rule of God in their individual lives here on earth and are looking for the consummation of his Kingdom at the end of the age.

The First Five Beatitudes

The beatitudes, for example, make it abundantly clear that the precepts and teaching of the Sermon set an altogether impossible standard for anyone who has not experienced a radical conviction of sin and supernatural work of re-generation. The Sermon has been described as 'a perfect picture of the life of the Kingdom of God' here on earth; for although that kingdom has certainly not yet been consum-mated – and will, in fact, only be consummated by divine intervention – it has already come in a personal sense in the life of all those in whose hearts Christ is enthroned as King. Even so, the teaching of the Sermon continually searches our consciences and humbles us. As Martyn Lloyd-Jones has justly said: 'These Beatitudes crush me to the ground. They show me my utter helplessness . . . There is nothing that so leads to the Gospel and its grace as the Sermon on the Mount' (*Sermon*, I, p. 18).

In any attempt to interpret and apply the detailed precepts of the Sermon, he insists, it is of supreme importance always to remember that it is 'a description of character' rather than 'a set of rules and regulations'. To take some of its individual injunctions as a 'mechanical rule' to be applied indis-criminatingly, in every circumstance, would make them either 'ridiculous' or 'impossible'. Instead, these precepts and injunctions are descriptions and illustrations of the sort of persons Christians ought to be – persons who will in fact readily and whole-heartedly behave in this way in every situation in which they believe this is 'God's will and for his glory'. This means that whenever we find ourselves 'arguing' with these precepts, this must mean one of two things: there must be something wrong either in us ourselves or else in our interpretation of the Sermon. In the first case, our whole spirit may be wrong because it is not attuned to the Beatitudes or *willing* to behave accordingly. In the second, we may be misunderstanding the meaning and proper application of teaching which was intended to set out basic criteria for the life of *every* Christian (Lloyd-Jones, *Sermon*, I, pp. 28ff., 33ff.).

It was not by chance, therefore, that the first beatitude declares: 'How blest are those who know their need of God ['are poor in spirit']: the kingdom of heaven is theirs' (Matt. 5:3) – for this is the key to all the rest. The fundamental fact is that it is only those who realise their 'poverty' who can ever enter the Kingdom. This first beatitude teaches us that we can never deserve or earn our salvation, and that we can never, of ourselves, live according to the Sermon. Anyone who genuinely tries to do so will very soon realise how 'poor' he is. Entrance into God's Kingdom, and the ability to measure up in any real sense to its demands, is all of God's grace, not human merit.

It is a grave mistake to think that the reference here is to the financially 'poor' in general, or to those Christians who take a vow of 'poverty' as constituting a sort of spiritual elite, as a superficial view of the form of this beatitude found in Luke 6:20 (which reads 'How blest are you poor' [or 'you who are in need'], without any addition) might suggest – for Luke's version must be taken in its total context. He certainly tells us that Jesus read 'from the scroll of the prophet Isaiah', in the synagogue at Nazareth:

The Spirit of the Lord is upon me because he has anointed me;
He has sent me to announce good news to the poor,
To proclaim release for prisoners and recovery of sight for the blind;
To let the broken victims go free,
To proclaim the year of the Lord's favour,

and then sat down and said: 'Today in your very hearing this text has come true' (Luke 4:16–21). But the Hebrew word for 'the poor' in this quotation is translated 'the meek' in the A.V. and R.V., and 'the humble' in the N.E.B., while the word from the same root translated 'poor' in Isaiah 66:2 in the A.V. is rendered 'humble' in the R.V. and N.I.V., and is immediately followed by the words 'and contrite in spirit, and trembles at my word' (R.S.V. and N.I.V.).

It is true that in the Old Testament the 'poor' and 'humble' are often depicted as those who put their confidence in God alone; that welcome into God's Kingdom is emphatically *not* on the basis of wealth, privilege or merit, all of which are apt to prove spiritual debits rather than assets; and that when the Kingdom is consummated all poverty, sorrow and bondage – and, indeed, sickness, affliction and death – will be finally banished. But the basic thrust of this beatitude is that in this life it is a sense of spiritual bankruptcy and utter dependence on God which is indispensable to all those who would accept his kingly rule and live as his loyal subjects. It was tax-collectors and prostitutes who entered the Kingdom 'ahead' of those who were self-satisfied and proud (Matt. 21:31f.). A. W. Tozer summed this up admirably when he wrote:

> The way to deeper knowledge of God is through the lonely valleys of soul poverty and abnegation of all things. The blessed ones who possess the Kingdom are they who have repudiated every external thing and have rooted from their hearts all sense of possessing. These are the 'poor in spirit'. They have reached an inward state paralleling the outward circumstances of the common beggar in the streets of Jerusalem; that is what the word 'poor' as Christ used it actually means (*Pursuit*, p. 23).

The second beatitude reinforces this point when it declares: 'How blest are the sorrowful; they shall find consolation'. Clearly there is nothing particularly happy or 'blest' about one who mourns, is sorrowful or weeps (Matt. 5:4; Luke 6:21), unless this results from a deep sense of his own sin and unworthiness – and also, of course, of the sins and sorrows of others and of humanity in general. This second beatitude, when understood in this way, flows naturally from the first. For this is, in fact, 'the second stage of spiritual blessing. It is one thing to be spiritually poor and acknowledge it; it is another to grieve and mourn over it. Or, in more theological language, confession is one thing, contrition is another' (Stott, *Counter-culture*, p. 41). It was those who 'mourned' their own and their nation's sin to whom the Messiah was to bring 'garlands instead of ashes, oil of gladness instead of mourners' tears, a garment of splendour for the heavy heart' (Isa. 61:2ff.).

Today, however, most of us hanker after short cuts. Evangelists call for men and women to 'decide for Christ' or 'accept Christ' with very little emphasis on the fact that repentance normally *precedes* true conversion; and we hope to experience the power of Christ's resurrection without having to 'share his sufferings, in growing conformity with his death' (Phil. 3:10). To quote Tozer again:

> Come near to the holy men and women of the past and you will feel the heat of their desire after God. They mourned for Him, they prayed and wrestled and sought Him day and night, in season and out, and when they found Him the finding was all the sweeter for the long seeking ... Complacency is a deadly foe of all spiritual growth (*Pursuit*, p. 15).

The third beatitude, again, complements the first two: 'How blest are the meek [or 'those of a gentle spirit']; they shall have the earth for their possession' (Matt. 5:5). The Greek word translated 'meek' in this context – and, still more, when used by Jesus of himself in Matthew 11:29 – does not mean weak, spineless or self-deprecatory in a bogus or artificial way, but gentle, humble, considerate and unassuming (B.A.G.). The primary reference is to how a man thinks of himself and how he shows this in his attitude to others. It is people like this – and not the self-assertive, the aggressors, the go-getters, the people who parade their personality, or those who come to the top in the rat race – who will 'inherit the earth'.

The Greek word translated 'earth' in this verse also means

'land', and to Jewish ears the corresponding Aramaic term would probably have suggested the 'land of promise'. It seems that Jesus was in fact quoting from Psalm 37 that 'the humble shall inherit the land' and 'live there in peace for ever' (vv. 11 and 29). Whatever one's views on 'the Millennium' may be, it was almost certainly to the 'new heaven and new earth' (cf. Rev. 21:1ff.) that Jesus was referring when he told his disciples, in parabolic terms: 'Amen, I tell you: in the new age, when the Son of Man is seated on his throne in heavenly splendour, you my followers will have thrones of your own, where you will sit judging the twelve tribes of Israel' (Matt. 19:28).

Even in this world, however, it is those who have 'nothing' who in reality 'possess all things' (2 Cor. 6:10). The secret of this anomaly lies in our response to Jesus' invitation in Matthew 11:28 ff. to 'bend our necks' to his 'yoke' or lordship. Only so can we 'find relief' from the greed and competitiveness, or concern for our 'rights', position and reputation (and from the consequent resentment, frustration and disappointment) which make life a burden. The way of release is to go on learning from him; for, when our ambition is simply to do his will, we shall discover that his yoke does not chafe and the burden he lays upon us is light. That, presumably, is what it means to 'inherit the earth' even in this life.

These first three beatitudes are primarily negative in their approach, but with the fourth beatitude the emphasis passes decisively to the positive. 'How blest are those who hunger and thirst for righteousness' (Matt. 5:6) can, of course, be understood in the double sense either of longing for one's personal right standing with God and holiness of life, or of passionate concern for public morality and social justice – as the phrase 'to see right prevail' in the N.E.B. translation indicates. But, while the teaching of Jesus (including the Sermon) certainly provides the basis for social as well as personal ethics, the promise in this verse that those who hunger and thirst for righteousness will be 'filled' or 'satisfied' seems to me to indicate that it is the personal application which is basic.

Jesus himself taught that this 'righteousness', together with the 'happiness' or peace of heart that it engenders, may be thought of in what we may term three phases. The first of these is the right standing with God which is the very basis of the new covenant that was to be sealed with his blood 'shed for many for the forgiveness of sins' (Matt. 26:28). It is because of this alone that the repentant sinner, like the tax-collector in the parable, can be 'justified' (Luke 18:14). The second is our continuing response to his command to 'set your mind on God's Kingdom and his righteousness' (or 'justice'), the result of which is freedom from temporal anxieties (Matt. 6:33f.). And the third phase will be reached only when the King comes in power and glory (Matt. 24:30); for then all 'causes of stumbling' will cease to trouble us or others (Matt. 18:7), and his people will – as he promised – 'be with me where I am' (John 17:24) and will 'eat and drink at my table in my kingdom' (Luke 22:30).

The fifth beatitude, again, is positive rather than negative in its thrust: 'How blest are those who show mercy; mercy shall be shown to them' (Matt. 5:7). The primary reference here, however, seems to be to a man's disposition rather than the actions which express it; so it is probably better to retain the more usual rendering of the first clause, which commends – or, indeed, congratulates – 'the merciful'. In the New Testament the word 'mercy' is very seldom used in English translations for God's redemptive love in pardoning sin, which is commonly referred to as his 'grace'; instead, it almost always expresses his compassion or pity for man in his suffering, misery and wretchedness (largely, of course, as a result of sin – whether his own, that of others, or the entail of a sinful world).

The basic meaning of another word, regularly translated 'compassion', is vividly portrayed in the parable Jesus told about the Good Samaritan (Luke 10:30–7) who, when he saw a man (almost certainly a Jew) who had been robbed, stripped, beaten up and left lying by the roadside, took pity on him, tended his wounds, transported him to an inn, and paid for his keep and care. The poignancy of this illustration of 'mercy' or 'compassion' is greatly enhanced not only by the traditional hostility between Samaritans and Jews, but also by the behaviour of the priest and Levite who had, just previously, 'passed by on the other side'. Suppose the victim had been a member of the I.R.A., and his benefactor an ardent Orangeman, in Ulster today!

The theological problem in this beatitude is posed by the meaning and implications of the promise that 'mercy shall be shown to them'. From this some have argued that those who show mercy to others here on earth can be assured of God's mercy on the day of judgment, or even that to be good and kind is a prerequisite of salvation. Any such inferences would run directly counter to the fundamental teaching of the New Testament that salvation is a gift that cannot be earned, and that it is not those who are naturally good who qualify for regeneration but regeneration which enables a man to begin to live out the new nature he has received.

It may be asked, however, if this 'fundamental teaching' can really be sustained in the light of the 'parable of the Kingdom' recorded in Matthew 18:23–35, in which 'a king decided to settle accounts with the men who served him'. One of them owed him a gigantic debt that he could not possibly pay, so the king 'ordered him to be sold to meet the debt, with his wife, children and everything he had'. The man 'fell prostrate at his master's feet' and begged him to be patient – and the king 'was so moved with pity that he let the man go and remitted the debt'. No sooner had he gone out, however, than he met a fellow servant who owed him what was, comparatively speaking, a trifling debt, gripped him by the throat and demanded payment; whereupon precisely the former scene was re-enacted in reverse. But the first servant refused the identical entreaty he had himself made, and had his debtor jailed. When this was reported to the king he summoned him, reminded him that 'I remitted the whole of your debt when you appealed to me', and asked him if he was not 'bound' to show his fellow servant the same pity that he had himself been shown. So he 'condemned the man to torture until he should pay his debt in full'. And Jesus concluded the parable with the words: 'And this is how my heavenly Father will deal with you, unless you forgive your brother from your hearts'.

I do not think that this parable really runs counter to the

fundamental principles I have mentioned above. It is immediately obvious that this story, couched in terms of an oriental despot, is an outstanding example of the difference between a parable and an allegory (cf. pp. 39f., 56 above); and in this case the details certainly cannot be 'allegorised'. What it does do is to emphasise the fact that, while forgiveness can never be earned or deserved, it *must* be 'received' – and that a *sine qua non* of its reception is repentance. As C. F. D. Moule finely puts it:

> However eager the forgiver may be to offer forgiveness, it cannot be received, and reconciliation cannot be achieved, without repentance. But repentance cannot earn the forgiveness or make the recipient worthy of it, for, by definition, forgiveness is always an act of unearned generosity.[2]

The reason why forgiveness is conditioned by repentance is, he insists, 'because reconciliation is a personal relationship, and cannot be achieved without responsiveness'. So a 'simple but fundamental distinction' can be drawn, in the matter of forgiveness, 'between deserts and capacity'. Thus Jesus could claim, in the story recorded in Luke 7:36ff. about the 'woman who was living an immoral life', that the love she had expressed by washing his feet with her tears, drying them with her hair, kissing them and putting expensive perfume on them, demonstrated that she had already been forgiven – not that her love had *earned* this forgiveness.[3]

We must return to the subject of forgiveness later, but the connection between the principle discussed above and the fifth beatitude is, I think, obvious. The composite description of what a Christian is or should be, which is provided by the beatitudes as a whole, is not based on those human qualities which some men and women possess, in some degree at least, by nature, but on the transformation of character which is being effected by divine grace in those who have repented, received the Gospel and become new creatures. Thus, in the case of this particular beatitude, it is only an appreciation of our desperate need for mercy (as seen in the first beatitude), and then of the wonder of the mercy that has in fact been shown to us in Christ and the Gospel, that can, and by God's grace will, make us merciful.

The Last Three Beatitudes

The sixth beatitude is one of the best known and most searching verses in the Bible: 'How blest are those whose hearts are pure; they shall see God' (Matt. 5:8). This always links up in my mind with a verse in the Old Testament which came to mean a great deal to me at one period in my life. In the vivid phraseology of the A.V. this reads: 'For the eyes of the Lord run to and fro throughout the whole earth, to show himself strong in the behalf of them whose heart is perfect before him' (2 Chron. 16:9). Here the N.I.V. translates the phrase 'perfect before him' as 'fully committed to him'. Perfection of accomplishment is obviously impossible for fallen human beings, but perfection of heart, in this particular sense, is something to which we can certainly aspire – although our verse suggests that 'the eyes of the Lord' have to search far and wide to find those who reach even this standard. It is twice recorded of King Asa that 'his heart was perfect with the Lord all his days' (1 Kings 15:14; 2 Chron. 15:17), although his accomplishments were far from perfect (cf. 2 Chron. 16:7, 10). By contrast, we read that King Amaziah 'did that which was right in the sight of the Lord, but not with a perfect heart' (2 Chron. 25:2).

The words 'perfect' and 'pure' are not, it is true, by any means synonymous, but in the sixth beatitude the term 'pure in heart' almost certainly has more than one meaning. Tasker, for example, understands it as signifying 'the single-minded, who are free from the tyranny of a divided self, and who do not try to serve God and the world at the same time' (*Matthew*, p. 62). This is much the same as having 'a heart perfect before him' in the sense we have just seen in certain Old Testament verses, and corresponds closely with what Jesus said about the 'single', 'sincere' or 'sound' eye which alone can give light to the body (Matt. 6:22), just as it is only a 'pure' heart which can enable us to 'see God'. That is why he insisted that 'No servant can be the slave of two masters; for either he will hate the first and love the second, or he will be devoted to the first and think nothing of the second. You cannot serve God and Money' (Matt. 6:24).

This emphasis on single-mindedness, when reinforced by the fact that the Greek word here translated 'pure' also means 'unalloyed' (cf. Rev. 21:18, 21) or 'unadulterated', presents a stark challenge to the mixed motives and desire for the esteem of men which so often characterise, and vitiate, our Christian service and devotions. No wonder Jesus charged his disciples: 'Be careful not to practise your piety [charity, prayer and fasting] before men in order to attract their attention; for then you will have no reward from your Father in heaven' (Matt. 6:1). There is no contradiction between this verse and the command in Matthew 5:16 to 'Let your light so shine before men that, when they see the good you do, they may give praise to your Father in heaven'. The acid test is whose honour we desire: our own, or God's.

Jesus obviously did not intend to forbid, or discourage, public prayer, for in teaching his disciples how to pray he gave them, as an outline or example, what we call 'the Lord's Prayer', which was clearly phrased in terms of corporate prayer. What he did deprecate, whether in charity, fasting or prayer, was any ostentation or unreality (Matt. 6:2, 5, 16). But the words 'pure in heart', when taken as a composite phrase, clearly point also to the overriding emphasis Jesus always put on inward, moral purity rather than outward, ceremonial cleanness. This was the substance of many of his denunciations of the Pharisees (cf. pp. 46f. above). He even told them that 'You shut the Kingdom of Heaven in men's faces; you do not enter yourselves, and when others are entering, you stop them ... You travel over sea and land to make one convert; and when you have won him you make him twice as fit for hell as you are yourselves' (Matt. 23:13ff.). So they were 'like tombs covered with whitewash; they look well from outside but inside they are full of dead men's bones and all kinds of filth' (Matt. 23:27).

Yet it is noteworthy that in Matthew's Gospel it is immediately after this scalding denunciation of religious hypocrites in the words 'You snakes, you viper's brood, how can you escape being condemned to hell?' (Matt. 23:33) that we find the heart-broken lament: 'O Jerusalem, Jerusalem, the city that murders the prophets and stones the messengers sent to her! How often have I longed to gather your children, as a hen gathers her brood under her wings, but you would not let me' (Matt. 23:37).

The promise to the pure of heart is that 'they shall see God'. All down the ages this has been regarded by Christians as the *summum bonum*, or the acme of spiritual bliss. Here in this world we 'see God' with the eye of faith, primarily 'in the face of Jesus Christ' (John 14:9, 19–23; 2 Cor. 4:6) as revealed in the Bible – but also, of course, in other Christian lives, in nature, in history, and in the 'providence' which alone makes sense of our multi-textured experience of life. In heaven we shall see Christ in his glory (John 17:24; 1 John 3:2), with the veil of sin, unbelief and self finally removed; yet even in heaven, as it seems to me, it is in the face of Christ that we shall see the invisible, triune God. It will, however, be the *triune* God whom we shall see in him, so we can still sing:

> Father of Jesus, love's reward
>   What rapture will it be,
> Prostrate before thy throne to lie
>   And gaze and gaze on thee!

– remembering, of course, that one of the wonders of heaven will be that we shall be able to worship and serve, to be contemplative and active, at the same time.

Even in this life most of us must confess that we live very far below the experience Jesus promised us if we would obey him. John records that he said: 'The man who has received my commands and obeys them – he it is who loves me; and he who loves me will be loved by my Father; and I will love him and disclose myself to him ... Anyone who loves me will heed what I say; then my Father will love him, and we will come and make our dwelling with him' (John 14:21ff.). On these verses Tozer comments:

> As we begin to focus upon God the things of the spirit will take shape before our inner eyes. Obedience to the word of Christ will bring an inward revelation of the Godhead . . . A new God-consciousness will seize upon us and we shall begin to taste and hear and inwardly feel the God who is our life and our all (*Pursuit*, pp. 53ff.).

If the sixth beatitude is primarily concerned with an individual in himself – that is, in his singleness of purpose and personal purity – the seventh makes it clear that this attitude and character will show itself in his public behaviour. It is a natural, and very necessary, transition: necessary, because the man who is single-minded and whole-hearted can all too easily become narrow-minded and intolerant of others; natural, because one who 'sees God' must be progressively changed into his likeness, and God is the supreme peacemaker. This, presumably, is why the promise that corresponds to 'How blest are the peacemakers' is that 'they shall be called sons of God' (Matt. 5:9) – which may mean either that they will be recognised by others as sons of their heavenly Father because they bear his family likeness, or – with the N.E.B. – that 'God shall call them his sons', as persons who behave accordingly.

Peacemaking, like 'charity', must 'begin at home'. To attempt to bring third parties from enmity or alienation to reconciliation without a radical attempt to remove any discord in one's own relationship with others would represent the sort of hypocrisy to which Jesus referred, later in the Sermon, in his vivid picture of a man who offers to take a speck of sawdust out of his brother's eye without first removing a 'great plank' out of his own (Matt. 7:3ff.). Where the fault is, to *any* degree, our own, this means that we cannot enjoy an unclouded relationship with God until we do all we can to put matters right. Jesus taught this, in the vivid and categorical terms that are characteristic of this Sermon, when he said: 'If, when you are bringing your gift to the altar, you suddenly remember that your brother has a grievance against you, leave your gift where it is before the altar. First go and make peace with your brother, and only then come back and offer your gift' (Matt. 5:23f.). Obviously enough, this may be physically impossible or otherwise beyond our power; but we must at least resolve to do all we can, and feel genuinely contrite that we cannot do more. And even where we sincerely believe that the fault is wholly that of the other party, we cannot enjoy God's forgiveness of our own sins and shortcomings, as we have seen, while we harbour an unforgiving spirit – as Jesus made clear when he taught us how we should pray as a family.

In trivial matters, I believe, we can – and should – forgive our 'brother' from our hearts, for a 'grievance' of which he may not even be conscious, without further ado. Even in the case of something much more serious, we saw in our last chapter that Jesus forbids any personal retribution, enjoins a willingness to suffer wrong, and makes us think deeply about the propriety of self-defence or legal proceedings.

There are some circumstances, however, in which it is not possible to restore full fellowship with a fellow Christian without going to 'take the matter up with him', strictly between ourselves. If he will listen we shall have 'won [our] brother' over (as Jesus taught, in another context) and avoided any public breach. If private reasoning fails, we are then to call in 'two or three witnesses' to establish the facts and attempt conciliation. And if this, too, is ineffective, the rift will have become one that the local Christian fellowship should deal with; and anyone who then remains obdurate must be regarded as having excluded himself from that fellowship.[4]

Forgiveness is a two-sided matter: it must not only be offered, but also received (cf. pp. 108f. above). We are called to a humble, costly and generous attempt to make peace, but not 'peace at any price'. We are not at liberty to abandon any *genuine* principle; although the history of the Church proves that we are sadly prone to declare that any dispute or division is a matter of principle or doctrine rather than personality or obduracy, and Vatican II was certainly right when it declared that there is a 'hierarchy of doctrines', some much more important than others. 'Compromise' is, no doubt, a dirty word when it refers to essentials; but to meet one's brothers half-way, or more than half-way, in everything else is the way of love.

It seems clear that the basic thrust of this beatitude is directed to peace-making between man and man. But the fact that peacemakers are to be recognised as 'sons of God' reminds us that God's own peacemaking consisted in 'reconciling' men first to himself and then to one another. This was something even God could do only at great cost; for Jesus taught that it was by his life-blood that the new covenant was sealed (Matt. 26:28), and only when he had been 'lifted up' that he would be able to 'draw all men' to himself (John 12:33). It was not until he had died and risen again that he could explain this in a way which his disciples could even begin to understand (cf. John 16:12), but the fact that the apostolic Church did come to proclaim this 'mystery' is clear from Paul's statements that 'when we were enemies to God, we were reconciled to him by the death of his Son' (Rom. 5:10); that God had not only 'reconciled us men to himself through Christ', but had 'enlisted us in this service of reconciliation' (2 Cor. 5:18); and that Christ himself 'is our peace'.

> Gentiles and Jews, he has made the two one, and in his own body of flesh and blood has broken down the enmity which stood like a dividing wall between them; for he annulled the law with its rules and regulations, so as to create out of the two a single new humanity in himself, thereby making peace. This was his purpose, to reconcile the two in a single body to God through the cross ... (Eph. 2:14f.)

So a Christian peacemaker should do his utmost to remove 'enmity' of any sort, whether between himself and others, third parties, communities or nations. But he must remember three things. First, that Jesus said that in one sense he himself had not come 'to bring peace, but a sword', since even the most intimate family relationships would be put at risk when the persons concerned were divided in regard to their allegiance to him (Matt. 10:34ff.). Second, that peace follows in the wake of 'righteousness' (Isa. 32:17; cf. Matt. 6:33), not vice versa. Third, that it is only in Christ and his atoning death that 'love and fidelity have come together; justice and peace join hands' (Ps. 85:10). Ultimately, there is no other sure foundation for peace – whether personal, communal or cosmic.

The eighth beatitude differs from the first seven in that it does not describe the character and conduct of the Christian as such, but the way in which other people are likely to react to his character and conduct. In one sense this beatitude – as always – is closely linked with the one which directly precedes it, while in another sense it refers back to the earlier beatitudes as a whole. Its immediate linkage arises from the fact that one who does not return evil for evil, and does his utmost to live at peace with all men, is clearly vulnerable to exploitation; that the way in which he may at times feel that fellowship with another person cannot be fully restored without some straight speaking will often be resented; and that his attempts to reconcile third parties who are at enmity with each other are as apt to incur opprobrium as gratitude. But the fact that the promise attached to this beatitude – 'the Kingdom of Heaven is theirs' – is identical with that of the first beatitude clearly shows that it rounds off the sequence as a whole.

It is obviously vital to note that it is only 'those who are persecuted for righteousness' who are said to be 'blest', not those of us who receive treatment we may well deserve. Jesus made this very clear in the way in which he applied this beatitude to his disciples, in the next two verses, in terms of their suffering insults and 'every kind of calumny for my sake'. Thus it is only those who suffer persecution which they do not deserve, but which results from their allegiance and witness to him, whom Jesus bids to 'accept it with gladness and exultation, for you have a rich reward in heaven'. We need to remember that there are many parts of the world where Christians are today suffering bitter persecution for their faith, and that it is distinctly possible that this may be true of us in years to come.

The Character and Life-style of a Christian

As we have noted more than once in passing, these beatitudes may be said to sum up the character which *should* always mark a Christian, and which *must* be true of him, in some measure, if he is really a Christian at all. But the beatitudes do not only distinguish a Christian in a positive sense; they also distinguish him sharply, in a negative sense, from a non-Christian. Many people who make no religious profession whatever, it is true, are much more humble-minded, gentle, merciful and peace-loving than the generality of men, whether by natural disposition or as a result of enlightened self-discipline; far more so, indeed, than many of those who turn to Christ for salvation. After all, Jesus himself unequivocally declared that he had 'not come to call the righteous, but sinners'. The characteristics described in the beatitudes do not represent a Christian's natural disposition, or gifts of God's 'common grace', but the supernatural transformation that God begins to effect in all those who, under the influence of the Holy Spirit, recognise their spiritual poverty, sorrow over their individual and corporate sinfulness, accept God's estimate of their condition, and hunger and thirst for the righteousness he alone can give.

Throughout the whole Sermon Jesus contrasts the character and life-style to which he summons his disciples with that of both contemporary 'pagans' and Jewish religious leaders. Precisely the same contrasts subsist in 'Christendom' between those whose goal is riches, pleasure, self-fulfilment, dominance and success, on the one hand, and those of us who profess and call ourselves Christians, but all too easily adopt the same postures and values, on the other. We shall never perfectly attain to the exceedingly exacting standards of the Sermon until the eschatological Kingdom is established; but these characteristics must, progressively, distinguish all those who have, here and now, submitted to God's kingly reign. It is significant that an excellent book by John Stott on 'the message of the Sermon on the Mount' is aptly entitled *Christian counter-culture.*

In Matthew 5:13-16 Jesus emphasised that this 'counter-culture' was not to be cultivated in the seclusion of a cloister but in the ordinary life of the world. His disciples were to be both 'salt to the world' and 'light for all the world': that is, to act as a preservative to counteract the moral corruption that has been present in human society ever since the Fall, and as a lamp to illuminate its spiritual darkness. Something that looks like salt but has lost its pungency[5] can, however, neither preserve food from putrefaction nor give it the flavour it lacks, for it is of the essence of salt to be different from the fish or meat to which it is applied. Obviously enough, it can have no effect whatever if it is not in close contact with the food concerned; but unless it retains its distinctive qualities no proximity will avail. Otherwise it is 'good for nothing but to be thrown away and trodden under foot' (Matt. 5:13).

The tragedy is that many of us Christians are, to change the metaphor, strangely like chameleons who reflect the colour of our environment. We do this partly, like the chameleon, to escape notice and avoid embarrassment; but we also fondly imagine that this makes our Christian 'witness' more acceptable. We find it so difficult to be *in* the world but not *of* the world, and so easily forget that in this, as in all else, Jesus says: 'Come and learn from me' (Matt. 11:28ff.). He was the friend of tax-collectors and 'sinners'; he was welcomed to their company and their parties, and he could meet women of loose morals without embarrassment. He was certainly not a kill-joy whose attitude was sternly or exclusively negative, and people were 'amazed' by the 'gracious way in which he spoke' (Luke 4:22). But we cannot imagine him lowering his standards or hiding his real self; and he could – and did – rebuke religious hypocrites in the most scathing terms. In him 'grace and truth' were uniquely combined (John 1:14).

So Jesus in teaching his disciples used the metaphor of light as well as salt. But just as salt cannot act as a preservative unless it is in close contact with the fish or meat it is intended to preserve, so a lamp can give little or no light if it is put 'under the meal-tub' instead of on the appropriate lamp-stand. Light, by definition, is fundamentally different from darkness; and a lamp which is covered up, even if it remains alight, cannot fulfil the purpose for which it was made by penetrating and illuminating the darkness that surrounds it. Precisely the same is true of Christians, Jesus taught. They were never to do acts of charity, pray or fast 'so as to be seen of men' and enhance their personal reputation (Matt. 6:1-8, 16ff.); but they must not try to hide their Christian life-style (Matt. 5:16).

As we have seen, there is no contradiction in this superficially different teaching. The basic distinction is whether the motive is that men should praise us, or glorify our 'Father in heaven'. To parade piety in religious circles is a very different thing from letting a Christian character and manner of life be seen, without ostentation, in a largely hostile world.

It is startling to note the emphasis, in both these metaphors, put on the initial word 'You'. Speaking to a little company of humble disciples, Jesus declared, in effect, that they – and, by implication, they only – could provide the antiseptic and enlightenment of which human society as a whole stood in such desperate need. Through them he says the same thing to his disciples today, when the need of the world takes an outwardly different form, but is fundamentally the same. Nor were these words addressed to the Church as an institutional body, but to individual Christians in their personal lives and witness (cf. Lloyd-Jones, *Sermon*, I, pp. 163ff.).

When we ask how this can be, the metaphor of light inevitably suggests the answer, for we are reminded that Jesus also said: 'I am the light of the world' (John 8:2). The individual Christian is the salt and light of the community in which he lives and of the people with whom he mixes, not primarily because he knows and communicates, when he can, the Gospel which exposes and illuminates the world's darkness – vitally important though this is – but because he is a tiny twig on one of the branches of the vine which is Jesus Christ himself (John 15:1ff.). He lives in the body of his Church, and in its most insignificant members, by his Spirit, and each of us finds his true life in him alone. It is the Holy Spirit, Jesus' *alter ego*, who will, in and through the Church and its members,

confute the world, and show where wrong and right and judgment lie. He will convict them of wrong, by their refusal to believe in me; he will convince them that right is on my side, by showing that I go to the Father when I pass from your sight; and he will convince them of divine judgment, by showing that the Prince of this world stands condemned ... He will glorify me, for everything that he makes known to you he will draw from what is mine (John 16:8-11, 14).

It is at this point that we must turn briefly to the teaching of Jesus about prayer. This will, no doubt, take its proper place in the book in this series on *The Example of Jesus*, for it is clear that Jesus taught his disciples, especially on this subject, much more by example than by precept. It is equally clear that it is only as the Christian waits before God that he can begin to measure up to the standard set by the beatitudes, or to realise in experience the blessings they promise.

In the teaching of Jesus the basic background and encouragement to true prayer is to know the character of God as Christ alone could reveal this (Matt. 11:27), and yet to dare, as Jesus himself habitually did, to approach him as 'Abba, Father'. To know his *character* should rid us of any idea that he will be deceived by an ostentatious prayer (Matt. 6:1, 5), or impressed by one of meaningless repetition ('babbling' in N.E.B.) or artificial prolongation (Matt. 6:7). It should also teach us that it is not always necessary to go into detail, since he knows what we need before we ask him (Matt. 6:8). To know him as our ever loving *Father* should enable us to pray in faith; for when we need bread we do not have to plead even with a fallible earthly father not to give us a stone, and still less a snake instead of a fish (Matt. 7:9-11).

Why, then, should we pray at all? First, because the God who has adopted us as his sons and daughters at such infinite cost in his eternal Son is not a remote, impassive deity but a heavenly Father who delights in our love and worship. It is our relationship with him that is fundamental – in prayer as in all else. Secondly, because to begin our prayers, as Jesus taught us (Matt. 6:9f.), with a heart-felt desire that God's name (or revealed character) should be venerated, his Kingdom consummated and his will done – both in our own lives and in the world at large – lifts our eyes and moulds our character. Thirdly, because to ask him to supply our daily need for sustenance, forgiveness and deliverance from evil reminds us of our utter dependence on him, helps us not to be anxious about, or too deeply interested in, such matters as our food and clothes (cf. Matt. 6:25-34), and brings home to us our duty to forgive others (Matt. 6:11-15) and not to lead them into temptation (cf. Matt. 18:6f.).

If God is our ever loving Father, why do we sometimes need to *go on* asking, seeking and knocking (Matt. 7:7f.; cf. Luke 11:5-8; 18:1-8)? This is not because he is reluctant to give, but because it is only prepared hearts that can value and receive his richest blessings. Again, why should we intercede for others, or pray 'the Lord of the harvest to send out workers into his harvest field' (Matt. 9:38)? Partly, no doubt, because this alerts us to, and keeps us mindful of, the needs of others; but also because the co-operation of his people in the mysterious battle between the Almighty and the powers of evil somehow releases spiritual resources in a way we do not now understand (cf. Mark 9:28).

Prayer *may*, Jesus taught, be addressed to him himself (John 14:13f.), but should normally, it seems, be to the Father in the name of the Son (John 15:16; 16:23f.). To pray in Jesus' name is not simply to make requests for his sake, but with his authority – which must mean as he himself would pray. So the abundant promises that our prayers will be answered (cf. Mark 11:24f.) are limited not only by the faith, motive and spirit of those who pray but also by the loving and omniscient will of the one to whom their prayers are addressed. Psalm 106:13-15 stands as an eternal warning about the spiritual impoverishment that may result from persistently demanding an affirmative answer to a petition that is not in accordance with our Father's perfect will.

When we think of the beatitudes primarily in terms of life-style rather than character, Luke's account of what is commonly called 'The Sermon on the Plain' may give us a slightly different slant from the summary Matthew gives of what was essentially the same teaching. Luke limits himself to four beatitudes, which correspond to the first, fourth, second and eighth, respectively, in Matthew's account; but Luke also adds four 'woes' to balance each of his beatitudes (Luke 6:20-6). What first strikes one about Luke's wording is that, although his last two beatitudes differ only in phraseology from Matthew's, his first two beatitudes seem, at first sight, to refer primarily to material rather than spiritual conditions. Thus in place of Matthew's 'How blest are those who know their need of God ['are poor in spirit']' Luke has 'How blest are you who are in need' without further qualification; and instead of Matthew's 'How blest are those who hunger and thirst for righteousness [or 'to see right prevail']', Luke has 'How blest are you who now go hungry'. Yet even here I am myself convinced that there is no fundamental difference[6] between these two very brief summaries of what must have been a much longer 'Sermon' in spoken form; for it is noteworthy that in Luke's account Jesus addressed all four beatitudes explicitly to his own disciples – and probably to the inner circle who had given up much to follow him (as the fourth beatitude seems to confirm by the words 'How blest are you when men hate you, when they outlaw you and insult you and ban your name as infamous, because of the Son of Man').

So it seems clear that Luke, like Matthew, did not regard poverty and hunger, *per se*, as particularly blest. But when Luke's first two beatitudes are taken together with his corresponding woes – 'But alas for you who are rich; you have had your time of happiness', and 'Alas for you who are well-fed now; you shall go hungry' (both of which are absent from Matthew, and appear to have been addressed to a considerably wider group) – it seems inescapable that, while the primary application of these beatitudes and woes is in spiritual rather than purely material terms, they point decisively to a Christian life-style which is modest and sacrificial rather than opulent and self-indulgent. Jesus clearly had a particular care for the poor and wanted his disciples to share his concern for social justice; and we dare not ignore his categorical statement: 'How hard it will be for the rich to enter the Kingdom of God!' (Mark 10:23).

It is a particular tragedy, therefore, that the Christian Church is missing such a unique opportunity in this respect today, when so many groups and individuals are turning in frustration and despair from the affluent life-style and materialistic culture of their seniors. Instead, they opt for a very different mode of life and try to find and propagate an alternative culture of their own. But the only satisfying counter-culture was exemplified by Jesus, and adumbrated in this Sermon, nearly two thousand years ago.

In the final analysis a man's life-style depends on his convictions, and the character and perspectives these convictions generate. As Jesus himself put it: 'Here lies the test: the light has come into the world, but men prefer darkness to light' (John 3:19). On this Dr Lloyd-Jones has aptly commented: 'We always need something to show us the difference, and the best way of revealing a thing is to provide a contrast' (*Sermon*, I, p. 165). This is the message of the Sermon on the Mount.

Chapter 6

The Social Ethics of the Kingdom

My purpose in this chapter is to discuss the teaching of Jesus about a few points which fall within the sphere of social rather than personal ethics. In some cases this teaching must be deduced from a short, seminal saying, almost epigrammatic in form, which is recorded in the Gospels as the quintessence of his reply to a question or questions put to him by others. Elsewhere, it often has to be inferred from a number of scattered statements reported in a variety of contexts.

Church and State

We shall begin with what is probably the most famous of all the apophthegmatic 'sayings' recorded in the Gospels: 'Render to Caesar the things that are Caesar's, and to God the things that are God's.'[1] This logion is accepted as authentic by the great majority of scholars, including Bultmann.[2] All three Synoptists record it, not as a pregnant aphorism pronounced *in vacuo*, but as Jesus' magisterial conclusion to his handling of a very crafty question, put to him by an uneasy alliance of mutually incompatible critics rather than honest enquirers. The three accounts differ only in minor details.

His questioners, Mark reports, were 'a number of Pharisees and men of Herod's party' – an unnatural partnership at any time, and particularly so in regard to the exceedingly vexed issue about which they were to ask his opinion (Mark 12:13). The plot was actually hatched, Luke states, by the 'lawyers and chief priests' (Luke 20:19) – a phrase which probably refers to the Sanhedrin or a group of its members; and the questions they came to ask were: 'Are we, or are we not, permitted to pay taxes to the Roman Emperor? Shall we pay or not?'

The first of these questions represented a theological problem concerning which they asked Jesus to give a rabbinical ruling on the correct interpretation of the Jewish law on this subject, while the second (which only Mark records) was overtly political. The chief priests and the Herodians would have said 'Yes' to both points; but the Pharisees, together with the majority of the populace, were fundamentally opposed to the Roman occupation and paid the imperial taxes only by compulsion. If, then, Jesus had answered both questions in the affirmative, the Pharisees would have been able to belittle his patriotism and fidelity to Jewish traditional teaching in a way calculated to lose him popular support and even perhaps to alienate those of his disciples who had a Zealot background (cf. Mark 3:18); whereas a negative answer, particularly to the second question, would have provided the chief priests with evidence on which they could bring a charge of sedition or treason against him before the Roman governor – as, we are told, they subsequently did (Luke 23:2), but without any evidence to support it. This would put his life itself at risk, rather than merely his following and reputation; so the question was introduced, as all the Synoptists record, in a way which virtually invited such an answer.

'Teacher', they said, 'you are an honest man, we know, and truckle to no one, whoever he may be'. But Jesus saw through their plot and said: 'Why are you trying to catch me out?' He then told them to 'show' or 'fetch'[3] him a denarius (the silver coin in which the tribute or poll-tax to Rome had to be paid, rather than the copper coins[4] – with inscriptions much less offensive to Jewish sentiments – which were in common use in Palestine). In this way he forced them to reveal the fact that they had a denarius on their persons – or, in default, to go and fetch one – stamped with the bust of Tiberius and an inscription which, had it been spelt out in full, would have read:

'Tiberius Caesar Divi Augusti Filius Augustus' (the implication of which becomes even more explicit from contemporary Syrian coins, where its Greek form is 'Tiberios
Kaesar Theou Sebastou Huios Sebastos', which may be
translated: 'Emperor Tiberius, august Son of the august
God').[5]

When the coin was produced Jesus simply asked 'Whose
head is this, and whose inscription?'; and to that question there
was only one answer they could give, however reluctantly. It
was indubitably Caesar's. In the ancient world tribute was a tax
paid by subjugated nations; and by paying it the Jews
acknowledged not only the supremacy of Rome, but also the
financial, legal and economic system which, however much
most of them resented it, the Pax Romana maintained. 'Very
well then', Jesus said (according to the Lukan account), 'pay
[literally 'give back to'] Caesar what is due to Caesar, and pay
['give back to'] God what is due to God'. The logic of this
formula left his questioners baffled, for it could not be
represented to the Roman authorities as treason, nor to the
people as a betrayal of their religion. But Jesus' reply was much
more than a brilliant evasion of an insidious trap; it
demonstrated 'his ability, in the momentary exchange of
controversy, to enunciate a principle which has proved to be
the basis of all future discussion of the problem of Church and
State' (Caird, *Luke*, p.222).

What, precisely, does this historic maxim mean? Obviously
enough, Jesus thereby recognised that a civil government has
the right, in principle, to levy taxes, and that citizens have a
corresponding duty to pay them. As Tasker puts it:

Both Caesar and God have their rights; therefore to pay
taxes to the one is not to rob the other of His due. This all-
important pronouncement of Jesus shows that He distinguished without dividing the secular and the sacred, and
that He united without unifying the two spheres in which His
disciples have to live. They are citizens of two cities, the
earthly and the heavenly, and they have duties to discharge
in both (*Matthew*, p. 210).

This is perfectly true, so far as it goes; but it does not go far enough. For it is evident, from the teaching of Jesus as a whole, that man's primary allegiance is to God alone. And it follows from this that the obedience a Christian owes to the civil power, within its rightful sphere, is itself part of his obedience to God.

Günther Bornkamm is mistaken when he asserts that this episode 'is the only scene in the Gospels where the problem of the power of the state is mentioned' (*Jesus*, p. 120); for John records that Jesus said to Pilate: 'You would have no authority at all over me if it had not been granted you from above' (John 19:11). In other words, a civil government has a God-given sphere in which it may act by divine delegation. Civil governments, however, sometimes exercise this delegated authority rightly, and sometimes wrongly; and when their legislation or their executive action clearly exceed their proper bounds, a Christian's absolute loyalty to God must prevail over his conditional loyalty to any human delegate. Far from there being a 'temporal', 'secular' or 'political' sphere that 'possesses an autonomy of its own or somehow stands outside God's creation' (as R.J. Cassidy[6] summarises a view other than his own), the fact is that 'God deals with man partly through the impersonal and fallible institutions of society and civil government, partly through the direct and personal impact of his own sovereign love' (Caird, *Luke*, p. 222).

It was in this way that the apostolic Church understood the teaching of Jesus. When, for example, the Sanhedrin categorically forbade the apostles to speak or teach in public in the name of Jesus, Peter and John replied: 'Whether it is right in the eyes of God for us to obey you rather than God is for you to judge. We cannot possibly give up speaking of things we have seen and heard' (Acts 4:18ff.). It is true that the Sanhedrin was not the civil government, but the Romans recognised its authority within its special sphere. The problem that inevitably faces us in all such cases, then, is to know when a civil government or ecclesiastical authority is properly performing God-given functions, and when, by contrast, it is going beyond its proper sphere or acting, even within that sphere, in a way which is contrary to God's will and is morally wrong. And in the latter circumstances there is a further problem, especially for a Christian: the point at which he may, or must, withhold his obedience or even his allegiance.

The answer given by the early Church to these questions can be inferred from Romans 13:1-7 and 1 Peter 2:13-17. The *moral* authority of a civil government, the apostles taught, was not to be located in force of arms, in a mythical 'social contract', in an elective process, or in some doctrine of historical, economical or psychological inevitability, but in divine institution. Its proper function was to act as God's agent for the public good, to punish criminals and to commend those who do right; and the corresponding duty of its subjects was to 'pay tax and toll, reverence and respect to those to whom they are due'.

It seems to be overwhelmingly probable that Jesus did himself pay the Roman poll-tax. But he certainly did not think that Herod Antipas, 'that fox' (Luke 13:32), deserved much respect, to say nothing of some of the religious leaders; and his warning to his followers that they would be brought before 'kings and governors' for his name's sake (Luke 21:12), and that they must not ape the 'lordship' that the 'kings of the Gentiles' exercised (Luke 22:24f.), must have included an implicit reference to Rome. Throughout the period of Paul's missionary journeys, however, Roman officials generally stood for justice as well as order; and as a Roman citizen he could (and did) appeal to them against mob violence, and to the Emperor himself against local intrigues, incompetence or corruption.

But what if the civil power were to turn its God-given functions upside down and begin to promote the evil and persecute the good? Would it not then forfeit – in part, at least – any right to obedience or allegiance? In a democracy there is always the theoretical possibility of amending offensive legislation, of calling arbitrary officials to account, and of ousting discredited governments. This should, indeed, be regarded not only as the citizen's right, but his duty. Yet the fact remains that democracy is no guarantee of social justice, for a duly elected majority government may oppress minority groups and resist all constitutional attempts to introduce legislative reforms or to influence executive action. So even in a democracy a Christian may feel compelled, in some circumstances, either to disobey the law or to resort to protests or demonstrations. In an autocracy his choice will be far more limited, and there may be no alternative to passive resistance or overt revolt. But at this point the further question arises whether the teaching of Jesus ever sanctions violence or the use of force – and, if so, in what circumstances? But before we turn to this difficult and controversial subject, there are a number of other points which demand attention.

First, a passing reference must be made to the incident, recorded in Matthew alone (17:24-7), in which Peter was asked: 'Does not your master pay temple-tax?' This half-shekel tax goes back to Exodus 30:11-16; so the reaction of Jesus to this question should, strictly speaking, be discussed in the context of his attitude to the Mosaic law, rather than to civil governments and their taxes. Matthew records that when Peter came into the house, Jesus forestalled him by saying: 'What do you think, Simon? From whom do the kings of the earth collect duty or taxes – from their own sons or from others?'; and some commentators (e.g. Hill, *Matthew*, p.271) take this question, together with Jesus' subsequent remark: 'Then the sons are exempt', as referring not only to the temple-tax but also to political power and taxes in general. It seems clear, however, that Jesus referred to 'the kings of the earth' in this context only by way of illustration, so his subsequent comment 'Then the sons are exempt' must presumably be taken as a somewhat oblique reference to whether the heavenly King required the temple-tax to be paid by his 'sons' of the 'new Israel'.

In order not to 'give offence' or 'cause difficulty' Jesus and his disciples paid this tax; and the apostolic Church probably continued to pay it until the Temple was destroyed – although, with the coming of him who was 'greater than the Temple' (Matt. 12:6) and his supreme sacrifice, the Temple and its ritual had ceased to have any real significance. Then, after the destruction of the Temple, this tax (Josephus tells us) was exacted from the

Jews by the Romans and devoted to the temple of Jupiter Capitolinus.[7] Christians presumably evaded or resisted this imposition when they could; but the generalisation that the words of Jesus in this context mean that Christians, 'because of their relation of sonship to God, the King of heaven . . . are free from obligations to the State' runs directly counter both to the teaching of Jesus about God and Caesar, and the way in which the apostles understood this teaching, as outlined and discussed above.

Marriage and Divorce

Jesus' logion about marriage and divorce, 'What God has joined together, man must not separate' (Matt. 19:6; Mark 10:9), is almost equally famous and even more controversial. But the essence of his teaching on this subject, as recorded in Matthew 5:31f. and 19:1-12, in Mark 10:2-12 and in Luke 16:18, is – I should have thought – clear beyond any reasonable controversy: namely, that God's plan and standard for marriage is life-long fidelity in a monogamous partnership. This is implicit in the fact that Jesus, quoting from both Genesis 1:27 and 2:24, insisted that God had 'from the beginning' made man male and female – in order that a married couple might form a unique, exclusive and lasting union, physical and spiritual (Gen. 2:18-24), which would transcend every other human relationship. Nothing less than this can be signified by the statement that a man would 'leave' his father and mother and 'cleave' to his wife in such a way that the two would 'become one flesh'. All too soon sinful human beings marred this plan, and lowered this standard, by adultery, polygamy and divorce.

So much is clear; it is after this that problems raise their heads. First, of whom, precisely, can it be truly said that God has joined them together? Not, surely, of a man who has intercourse with a prostitute, although Paul uses the phrase 'The pair shall become one flesh' even of such a relationship (1. Cor 6:16) in order to throw into stark relief what a perversion of God's intention for bodily and spiritual union such an act represents.[8] After all, even on the most literal interpretation, this could be true only of an act of intercourse in which both parties were previously 'virgins'. Nor, in my view, are the words 'what God has joined together' in any way exclusive to, or necessarily inherent in, what is often termed a 'sacramental' marriage. In its full sense the phrase can be applied today[9] only to those who enter into this relationship without constraint, deception or personal incapacity,[10] since any of these exceptions makes a marriage – even if contracted with the most solemn ritual – in principle[11] a nullity. Some commentators would go further than this, and remark that in some marriage relationships the parties signally fail to achieve 'the unity which could alone be truthfully described as "a joining together by God"' (cf. Tasker, *Matthew*, p. 181). But although there is a real sense in which this is true, it represents a very shaky foundation on which any 'law' of marriage could be based.

This question cannot really be considered in isolation from the still more difficult, and highly relevant, problems of divorce and the remarriage of divorced persons. Here, again, it seems clear that Jesus taught that the provision in Deuteronomy 24:1 (that a husband who 'dismissed' his wife must always give her 'a certificate of divorce') represented a regulation, in the interests of the discarded wife, of a practice of divorce which had its origin in the 'hardness' of men's hearts. There is no suggestion that Jesus had any doubt that this recognition of – and concession to – human frailty had been given by divine permission; but he clearly regarded the element of 'command' as applying only to the giving of the certificate, not the practice of divorce, which was, he affirmed, contrary to the original design of God. Even so, this concession to fallen humanity was limited to circumstances in which the husband found 'some uncleanness' in his wife – although it is true that Hillel and many of the Rabbis gave an exceedingly wide application to this phrase. As for the explicit command (in the next three verses in Deuteronomy 24) that, should the 'dismissed' wife remarry and then be widowed or again divorced, her former husband might in no circumstances remarry her,[12] this must be seen as a further restraint on frivolous divorce or a low view of marriage.

Commentators discuss at some length the obvious differences between the reports given in the three synoptic Gospels of what Jesus taught about whether divorce was still in any circumstances permissible and about the status of a subsequent marriage. Many scholars insist that Mark 10:2-12 and the brief reference in Luke 16:18 and 1 Corinthians 7:10f. forbid divorce – or, at any rate, divorce and remarriage – in absolute terms. So they explain Matthew 5:32 and 19:9 as introducing what has come to be known as 'the Matthean exception', in order to bring the teaching of Jesus closer to Jewish practice (and also, perhaps, to the casuistry of the Church from which this Gospel may have emanated), on the mistaken assumption that Jesus must have regarded divorce as permissible, in accordance with Deuteronomy 24:1, in a case of actual 'unchastity'[13] (the meaning that was given to the phrase 'some uncleanness' by Shammai and his followers, rather than some petty offence which would, in effect, give a husband licence to 'dismiss' his wife almost at his whim).

But this whole argument seems to me highly questionable. First, there is no manuscript evidence whatever for omitting this exception from Matthew 5 or 19. Second, even if it was not actually put into words by Jesus, it may well have been implicit; and Mark and Luke may have so understood the teaching they recorded. After all, the penalty prescribed in the Mosaic law for adultery by (or with) a married woman was death by stoning. When this penalty was exacted the marriage would obviously end with her death; and, where it was not, her infidelity may have been regarded as entailing the dissolution or 'death' of the marriage. But even if this view is accepted, it is clear that 'the Matthean exception' would not operate automatically, and would not be mandatory on the husband. Forgiveness would always be possible – and, surely, 'the more excellent way'; but divorce would, in these circumstances, be permissible.

Whatever the teaching of Jesus on this subject may mean for the Church and for individual Christians, it by no means follows that civil legislation should not make provision for the judicial dissolution of marriages which have, humanly speaking, irrevocably broken down. It is true that Jesus taught that life-long fidelity in monogamous marriage was God's intention for man as man, rather than Christians as such. But in the maxim 'What God has joined together, man must not separate [or 'put asunder']' the last phrase almost certainly refers to the parties to the marriage, not to a court of law – for in rabbinic teaching, even today, it is only the husband who can pronounce a divorce. To preclude any possibility of dissolving a marriage in civil law, on the basis of a dogma of transcendental indissolubility, even where the parties (to give an extreme example) have not only separated but are living with, and begetting illegitimate children by, other partners, is beneficial neither to the health of society nor the status of marriage. So I believe it is right for civil legislation to be so framed as to hold as equitable a balance as possible between upholding the stability of the marriage bond, providing for a decent burial for a marriage that is manifestly dead, and protecting the proper interests of both the parties and their children.

But what of the Church and its individual members? I have no doubt that a Christian should be ready to forgive a marriage partner who is guilty of adultery or cruelty, for example, and who then repents; but does this hold good if this conduct becomes habitual and there is no sign of any real repentance? To perpetuate such a situation may be disastrous for the children. The alternative is either separation or divorce; and under the present law the first of these alternatives may well lead to the second. Even before the principle of the 'matrimonial offence' was widely discarded in favour of that of the irreversible breakdown of marriage as the criterion for civil divorce, it was, moreover, very doubtful whether a Christian would have been right to persist in refusing a divorce to a spouse who begged to be allowed to legitimate another *de facto* union – however firmly the Christian concerned held to his or her marriage vows.

Again, is the remarriage of the 'innocent party' inevitably

'adulterous'? One difficulty here, of course, is to define the term 'innocent party', since in practice the commission of a 'matrimonial offence' is more often the result than the cause of a marital breakdown; and in this both parties are usually to some extent to blame. In the context of Jesus' teaching divorce meant the 'dismissal' of a wife by her husband[14] or the 'desertion' of a husband by his wife[15]; and the economic position of women virtually forced a divorced wife, in many cases, into prostitution or a second marriage (cf. Matt. 5:32; Luke 16:18).

Today, however, the circumstances in regard to divorce and remarriage have changed greatly. This is not in any way to detract from the solemnity of our Lord's words. But clearly, on a wholly literal interpretation, a second marriage during the life-time of the former spouse – except in the case of 'the Matthean exception' or 'the Pauline privilege' (cf. below), in which the marriage is thought of as itself dead – would normally represent a series of continuing acts of adultery. Logically, therefore, 'repentance' would involve either an attempt to put the clock back by dissolving the second marriage and resuming the first (which might well be impossible) or total abstinence from sexual relations in the second marriage; and I should have thought that the only practicable pastoral advice in such cases must be that, after a genuine repentance from the sins and failures of the past, everything possible should be done to avoid wrecking yet another marriage. But this means that, even if the second marriage is regarded as (in one sense) 'adulterous', an initial repentance must 'cover' the continuance of the union.

One further point remains. The Gospels preserve the teaching of Jesus on this subject only in a very summary form (cf. in particular Luke 16:18); and it seems clear that his teaching was often couched in trenchant, categorical terms which demand not only whole-hearted obedience but reverent elucidation and sensitive application. An illuminating example of this, in the context of our immediate problem, is provided by 1 Corinthians 7:12-16.

This passage shows that the apostle regarded even a pagan

marriage as a valid union. If, therefore, one of the parties subsequently became a Christian, he or she must not divorce the other – however incompatible marriage with a pagan partner might now prove – provided the non-Christian party was prepared to go on living with the Christian. 'But if the unbeliever leaves', Paul continued, 'let him do so. A believing man or woman is not bound in such circumstances' (1 Cor. 7:12f.). This must, surely, imply that the Christian would then be free to marry a fellow Christian; for it would be virtually meaningless merely to tell the Christian husband or wife that he or she was not 'bound' to continue a joint life that the other party refused to share! In other words, a second marriage in such circumstances would be valid and legitimate, rather than adulterous. Paul is careful to say that this is not an explicit command from the lips of Jesus, but he clearly believes that he is speaking under the guidance of the Spirit of God (cf. 1 Cor. 7:40). This so-called 'Pauline privilege' has been taken by Churches of the Reformed tradition to imply that wilful and protracted desertion of one party by the other, even in a marriage between two Christians, is so destructive of the very meaning and purpose of marriage as to make it *permissible* for the deserted party not only to claim a divorce but subsequently to remarry.

At first sight this ruling – and, *a fortiori*, its extension in Churches of the Reformed tradition – seems to run counter to the ruling Paul specifically attributes to Jesus himself in this same chapter. A wife is there charged not to 'separate herself from her husband', and told that, should she do so, 'she must either remain unmarried or be reconciled to her husband'; and the husband, on his part, is told that he 'must not divorce his wife' – presumably with the same implications (1 Cor. 7:10f.). The difference between this situation and that of 'the Pauline privilege' may, however, be not only that the latter involves a pagan husband who refuses to live with a partner who has become a Christian, but that in verses 10 and 11 the insistence is that neither wife nor husband must take the initiative in, or bear the responsibility for, breaking up a marriage[16] – as distinct from circumstances in which the other party makes the continuation of the marriage, in anything other than name, literally *impossible*. Even so, the last clause in Matthew 5:32 remains a problem.

Justice and Judgment

Turning next to social ethics in more general terms, we can again find in the teaching of Jesus a comprehensive maxim in the form of 'The Golden Rule'. In its Lukan form this reads: 'Treat others as you would like them to treat you' (Luke 6:31); whereas Matthew records it as 'Always treat others as you would like them to treat you, for this sums up the Law and the Prophets' (Matt. 7:12). The concept was not original, for it was already well known in its negative form in rabbinic writings and was cited by Hillel in the words: 'What is hateful to you, do not do to your fellow-creatures. That is the whole law; all else is explanation'. The major difference is that the negative form

is merely a rule of prudence; do not hurt other people lest they retaliate. The positive form is not prudential but absolute: this is how you are to treat others (positively), regardless of how they treat you. Jesus thus goes beyond the negative form, citing the rarer and more demanding form (Marshall, *Luke*, p.262).

This maxim can best be analysed, I think, in terms of the emphasis Jesus put on love, mercy and justice. He taught that the second part of the Decalogue can be summed up, in the words of Leviticus 19:18, as 'Love your neighbour as yourself' (Mark 12:31); he quoted Hosea 6:6 and said 'Go and learn what this means, "I require mercy, not sacrifice"' (Matt. 9:13); and he defined 'the more important requirements of the Law' (as distinct from meticulous hair-splitting about the payment of tithes on herbs and vegetables) as 'justice, mercy and faithfulness' (Matt. 23:23). Here justice means that impartial fairness which, like mercy and faithfulness, characterises God himself (cf. Acts 10:34) and which he looks for in his people

(Mic. 6:8). The corresponding passage in Luke reads: 'Alas for you Pharisees! You pay tithes of mint and rue and every garden-herb, but have no care for justice and the love of God' (Luke 11:42) – where the last phrase may mean either love for God (shown in faithfulness) or the love that God requires his people to show to all men. To be principally concerned with details of ceremonial observances rather than these basic moral qualities, on which the Old Testament prophets put such a major emphasis, was, Jesus said, to 'strain off a midge, yet gulp down a camel!' (Matt. 23:24).

It is important to remember that the Greek word (*krisis*) translated 'justice' above (and elsewhere, as in Matthew 12:20) is even more often translated 'judgment'. This meaning of the word is prominent in the teaching of Jesus himself – particularly in Matthew, where we read that he said:

> At the Judgment when this generation is on trial, the men of Nineveh will appear against it and ensure its condemnation, for they repented at the preaching of Jonah; and what is here is greater than Jonah. The Queen of the South will appear at the Judgment when this generation is on trial, and ensure its condemnation, for she came from the ends of the earth to hear the wisdom of Solomon; and what is here is greater than Solomon (Matt. 12:41f.).

Similarly, he is reported as saying that it would be more bearable on the day of judgment for Tyre and Sidon (Matt. 11:23; Luke 10:14) or for Sodom and Gomorrah (Matt. 10:15) than for those who refused to listen to his teaching or that of his messengers.

But although these passages, like Matthew 13:41f. ('so at the end of time the Son of Man will send out his angels, who will gather out of his kingdom everything that causes offence' – that is, all that is contrary to 'justice' in its widest sense – 'and all whose deeds are evil, and these will be thrown into the blazing furnace'), refer to the Great Assize at the Parousia, which is always depicted as ushering in both salvation and judgment, there was a present application too. 'Now is the hour of judgment for this world; now shall the Prince of this world be driven out', Jesus is reported as saying when he contemplated the imminence of the cross (John 12:31) – and he later taught that, when the Holy Spirit came in power, he would 'confute the world, and convince them of divine judgment, by showing that the Prince of this world stands condemned' (John 16:8 and 11).

It is clear that Jesus taught his disciples lessons in the sphere of social justice by example even more than by precept and admonition. His practical concern for the poor, sick, outcast and bereaved must have impressed itself deeply on their minds and consciences. He put a special emphasis on his mission to the destitute and oppressed; and it was from him that his disciples learnt the lesson that God had 'chosen those who are poor in the eyes of the world to be rich in faith and to inherit the kingdom he has promised to those who love him' (Jas. 2:5). In other words, the 'blessedness' of those who are literally poor, hungry or sad does not lie in their condition or circumstances as such, but in the promises that are specifically addressed to them.

Much the same, but in reverse, applies to the 'woes' in Luke 6:24-6. That pronounced on the rich is, explicitly, because they have 'already received [their] consolation' – presumably by hoarding or squandering their wealth, instead of treating it as a trust; those on people who are 'well-fed' and who 'laugh now' are, at least by implication, because they have lived in a sumptuous and irresponsible way, instead of sharing their provisions with others and taking life seriously; and that on the popular because, like the false prophets in the Old Testament, they have spoken 'smooth' things and have not witnessed to their Lord either by lip or life.

Poverty and Riches

In regard to wealth, the most stringent injunction of all was that addressed by Jesus to the rich man who came to ask him what he must do 'to win eternal life'. The story is told by all the

The Social Ethics of the Kingdom

Synoptists (Matt. 19:16ff.; Mark 10:17ff.; Luke 18:18ff.) with
very minor differences – except in regard to the initial form of
address and Jesus' response to this (cf. pp. 62 above). As we
have seen, in each account the question of eternal life is
equated, in the subsequent discussion between Jesus and his
disciples, both with entrance into the 'Kingdom' and with being
'saved'. It seems clear that the questioner expected Jesus to
specify some difficult or particularly meritorious task that he
must perform in order to gain his goal; but Jesus referred him
back to the Old Testament commandments, since he must have
known that perfect obedience to these carried the promise of
life (cf. Deut. 30:15-19; Ezek. 33:15; etc.). He replied that he had
kept all these from his youth; so what did he still lack? It was at
this point that Jesus challenged him, if he really wanted to go
the whole way, to sell his possessions, give to the poor, and
'come, follow me'. This reply was partly, no doubt, designed to
show him that he had not really 'kept all these'; for the fact that
he was not willing to dispose of his very considerable
possessions in favour of the poor proved conclusively that he
did not love his neighbour *as himself*. Again, Jesus may have
perceived that his possessions were an 'idol' which prevented
him from putting love for God uncompromisingly first in his
life.

However that may be, it is clear that Jesus did not teach that
all Christians should dispose of everything they possess, since
Luke records that there were certain women who provided for
him and his disciples 'out of their resources' (Luke 8:3), and
that Jesus declared that 'salvation' had come to the house of
Zacchaeus when he made a very generous, but by no means
total, distribution of his possessions to the poor (Luke 19:8f).
Like celibacy, it seems, total 'poverty' is only for 'those for
whom God has appointed it' (Matt. 19:11). But Jesus certainly
declared, to the amazement of his disciples, that it was
exceedingly difficult for a rich man to enter the Kingdom – so
difficult that he humorously likened it to a camel going
through the eye of a needle.

It was in fact impossible for him (or indeed for anyone else)
apart from the supernatural grace of God, which alone would

enable him to follow Jesus as a true disciple. And such
discipleship, Jesus insisted repeatedly, would necessarily mean
to 'deny [or 'disown'] himself and take up his cross' (cf. Mark
8:34) – a metaphor which would have been readily understood
in the Roman empire as meaning to regard himself as one who
had been sentenced to crucifixion. In some contexts this points
to a willingness to face literal martyrdom; in others to a self
denial that acts as though life in this world is 'already finished'
(cf. Marshall, *Luke*, p. 373).

Elsewhere, Jesus is reported to have told his disciples:
'Beware! Be on your guard against greed of every kind; a man's
life does not consist in the abundance of his possessions' (Luke
12:15). He then illustrated this fact by the parable of the Rich
Fool and added: 'This is how it will be for anyone who stores
things up for himself but is not rich towards God' (cf. Luke
12:16-21). Somewhat later in the same chapter Luke records
that Jesus exhorted his disciples to 'Sell your possessions and
give to the poor. Provide purses for yourselves that will not
wear out, treasure in heaven that will not be exhausted . . . For
where your treasure is, there your heart will be also' (Luke
12:33f.).

Again, he gave them a vivid illustration of the phrase we
have already noted about those who have 'already received
their consolation' by telling them the parable of Dives and
Lazarus, in which he depicted the rich man as one who 'feasted
sumptuously every day', while a poor man (whom he evidently
knew) 'who would have been glad to satisfy his hunger with the
scraps that fell from the rich man's table' lay at his very gate
(Luke 16:19-31). By contrast, Jesus said to one of his hosts:
'When you give a lunch or a supper, do not invite your friends
. . . or your rich neighbours; if you do, they may invite you back
and so you will be repaid. But when you give a party, invite the
poor, the crippled, the lame, the blind, and . . . you will be
repaid at the resurrection of the righteous' (Luke 14:12ff.).

Yet again, he showed how worldly wealth can be transmuted
into eternal gain by telling them the parable of the Unjust (or
'Prudent'?) Steward (Luke 16:1-9). According to the traditional interpretation of this parable, the steward first

squandered his employer's property and then, when given notice of dismissal, invited his master's debtors to falsify the promissory notes of their debts by a fraudulent reduction which would secure their good will in the future. But Duncan Derrett has plausibly suggested that these promissory notes probably included a substantial sum to represent interest for credit which was not acknowledged as such (which is a very common practice in legal systems in which interest on loans is forbidden); what the steward in fact did was to invite the debtors to re-write these notes in terms of the original debt alone (as the law would have properly required from the beginning). If this is the correct interpretation, as seems to me very likely from experience of such devices in the Islamic world, it makes it all the easier to understand why his master (or perhaps Jesus himself) 'commended' him for his prudence.[17] In any case, the emphasis falls on the lesson Jesus drew from the story when he said: 'So I tell you, use worldly wealth to gain friends for yourselves, so that when it comes to an end you will be welcomed into eternal dwellings' (by 'friends' who recognise their debt to the contributions made on earth towards their physical or spiritual needs in the form of funds given either for material relief or for evangelism). It was in this context that he declared that 'no servant can serve two masters', and insisted: 'You cannot serve both God and Mammon' (Luke 16:13).

Jesus also sent out his twelve disciples with the charge: 'Heal the sick, raise the dead, cleanse lepers, cast out demons. You received without cost; give without charge' (Matt. 10:8). He gave them authority to do what he himself was doing, for he insisted that 'It is not the healthy that need a doctor, but the sick; I did not come to invite virtuous people, but sinners' (Mark 2:17; cf. Matt. 9:12, Luke 5:31). It was his experience that 'tax gatherers and prostitutes' responded to his invitation more readily than did the Jewish religious leaders (Matt. 21:31). Thus he summed up his practice and teaching about social ethics in another well-known maxim: 'Be compassionate as your Father is compassionate' (Luke 6:36).

Social Reform, Violence and War

A brief allusion must also be made in this chapter to the teaching of Jesus about such subjects as slavery, polygamy, the status of women, and violence or the use of force. I say 'brief' advisedly, since his recorded teaching on these subjects is surprisingly scanty.

On slavery, the status of women in the ancient world or even polygamy as such, he is not in fact reported as making any direct comments whatever – although his attitude to polygamy, at least, is clear enough from his insistence that those whom God has joined together 'become one flesh', and from his consequent comments on divorce. As for slavery, the Greek word *doulos* is used indiscriminately in the New Testament for any type of servant; the institution of slavery was at that time universal; and any attempt to bring the practice to an abrupt end would have been wholly impracticable. But Jesus was eminently capable of making scathing comments on social evils regardless of whether there was any prospect of either their immediate amelioration or eventual abolition. Why then did he not speak out about the status of women and the institution of slavery?

A partial answer to this question can presumably be found in the fact that to have explicitly advocated such fundamental reforms in existing conditions would have diverted public attention (to say the least) from the supreme purpose of his mission, and would have made the task he bequeathed to his little band of politically powerless disciples utterly impossible. In addition it must be remembered that, as he himself repeatedly emphasised, he proclaimed only what was revealed to him, and positively commanded, by his heavenly Father (cf. p. 156 below) – and it is clear that God's hour for a social revolution of this dimension, with all the chaos and suffering that this would have involved then, had not yet struck.

Instead, Jesus gave the most unequivocal teaching, by example even more than by precept, about personal humility, and habitually showed both sympathy and respect for all those who were oppressed or under-privileged. He explicitly forbade his disciples to try to 'lord it' over one another; on the contrary, he insisted that 'the highest among you must bear himself like the youngest, the chief of you like a servant', for that was precisely the way in which he had himself come among them (Luke 22:25ff.). Elsewhere he taught that 'whoever does the will of my heavenly Father is my brother, my sister, my mother' (Matt. 12:50).

All these sayings (which could, of course, be multiplied) represent basic moral teaching that was to work, like yeast, secretly and gradually; but it is one of the major scandals of the Christian Church that, in spite of James 2:1-4, she has been so slow – and even unwilling – to understand or put into practice the implications of Jesus' teaching and example. Yet it can fairly be said that such social progress as has in fact been made – in the liberation of slaves, the founding of hospitals, the emancipation of women, the improvement of working conditions and the expansion of education – owes an incalculable debt to his life and teaching, and to the response (however belated and insufficient) of his followers.

In regard to violence or the use of force, we have already seen (pp. 91f. above) how categorically Jesus forbade his disciples to indulge in personal retaliation of any sort.[18] But I do not believe that this means that a Christian should stand idly by while a baby is kicked to death or a woman raped, for example. It is true that there is no explicit reference in the Gospels to physical intervention in defence of others; but I should have thought that this is covered by the general moral principles which Jesus explicitly or implicitly endorsed.

The only time when it is reported that Jesus himself had recourse to force was in the 'cleansing' of the Temple, where John states that he 'made a whip of cords and drove them out ... sheep, cattle and all. He upset the tables of the money changers, scattering their coins' (John 2:15). Here W. L. Lane goes considerably further than the evidence warrants when he comments that Jesus 'inflicted blows upon the guilty' (*Mark*, p. 404), while Joel Carmichael shows the absurdities to which unbridled fantasy can lead when he states that Jesus' greatest moment of triumph was his 'seizure and occupation of the temple in Jerusalem', when he 'drives out the priests, the merchants and holds the Roman garrison in check' (*sic*).[19] It is impossible to deny that in this 'cleansing' he used a degree of physical force to remedy what was both a theological and moral evil – for Jesus thus rid the Court of the Gentiles, albeit temporarily, 'of the obvious removable symbols of a Judaism that kept its temple to itself', and of a visible reminder that 'Gentile coins, as well as Gentile persons, were intolerable to the Jews in their temple'. In this light the phrase 'a robbers' cave' takes on a further significance: the condemnation of those who 'commit injustice' and deprive Gentiles of a welcome to 'a house of prayer' which was to be 'for all nations' (Marsh, *John*, pp. 148f.).

There are a few references to 'swords' in the Gospels which are apt to be misunderstood. One occurs in Luke 22:35-8 where Jesus, before going out to the Garden of Gethsemane, is recorded as reminding the apostles that he had previously sent them on an evangelistic mission 'without purse or pack', and then saying:

'It is different now; whoever has a purse had better take it with him, and his pack too; and if he has no sword, let him sell his cloak to buy one. For Scripture says, "And he was counted among the outlaws", and these words, I tell you, must find fulfilment in me,' ... 'Look, Lord,' they said, 'we have two swords here.' 'Enough, enough!' he replied.

Any idea that this incident implies that Jesus originally wished his disciples to resist his arrest can scarcely stand in view of the fact that two swords would certainly not have been 'enough' for this, and that, when Peter used one of them to cut off the right ear of the High Priest's servant, Jesus told him to desist and healed the stricken man (vv. 50f.). So Marshall is probably right in regarding Jesus' reference to the need for a purse and the indispensability of a sword as 'grimly ironical, expressing the intensity of the opposition which Jesus and the disciples will experience, endangering their very lives. They are summoned to a faith and courage which is prepared to go to the limit' (*Luke*, p. 823). In his own case, this meant to drink the cup the Father had given him (John 18:10f.). Matthew adds that Jesus not only told Peter to 'put up' his sword, but said: 'All who take the sword die by the sword' (Matt. 26:52).

This, again, is a difficult saying, since in its absolute sense it obviously is not true. It *may* have been said with a particular – and immediate – reference; but it seems more likely that it is a general maxim to the effect that violence provokes retaliatory violence. As such it may clearly be taken as a strong discouragement to both violence and war, but not as a categorical prohibition; for, on any interpretation of this episode, it is clear that the disciples were not rebuked for possessing two swords. It is in the teaching of the apostles, rather than of Jesus himself, that civil governments (rather than private citizens) are said to have the God-given duty to punish crime and commend virtue (Rom. 13:1-7; cf. 1 Pet. 2:13f.) – and thus 'hold the power of the sword'. But there is no reason to doubt that Jesus would have included a responsibly used 'police power' in the sphere delegated by God to 'Caesar'.

International and civil wars are, of course, a very different matter – particularly in the light of the horrendous weapons which exist today. But it must be recognised that no *direct* or unequivocal teaching of Jesus himself on this subject has come down to us. When Pilate asked Jesus whether he was a king, John reports that Jesus replied: 'My kingdom does not belong to this world. If it did, my followers would be fighting to save me from arrest by the Jews. My kingly authority comes from elsewhere' (John 18:36). This statement would certainly seem to exclude any sort of 'war of religion'. But in an evil world a national army may well be needed to reinforce the police in times of emergency. Jesus, again, is not reported to have said anything about soldiers as such, while John the Baptist apparently confined his message to them to the words: 'No bullying; no blackmail; make do with your pay!' (Luke 2:14.) It seems, moreover, that Jesus took the concept of war as one of the facts of life. It is recorded that he told his disciples:

When you hear the noise of battle near at hand and the news

of battles far away, do not be alarmed. Such things are bound to happen; but the end is still to come. For nation will make war upon nation, kingdom upon kingdom; there will be earthquakes in many places; there will be famines. With these things the birth-pangs of the new age begin (Mark 13-7f.; cf. Matt. 24-6; Luke 21:9).

This clearly does not mean that either wars or famines, for example, are not evil in themselves, and that everything possible should not be done to eliminate or control them. But is the invasion of another country *never* justified – even if, for example, it is to put a stop to genocide? And is resistance to enslavement *always* wrong? Questions such as these inevitably raise the basic moral problem of which is the lesser of two evils. Many people insist that any resort to arms whatever may lead to a holocaust, and that nothing could possibly be worse than that; whereas others feel equally strongly that there are some forms of brutality and ruthless exploitation that should be resisted at all costs. And if this is ever true, should a Christian always leave it to others to resist aggression or tyranny, however extreme? These are agonising questions to which no simple or categorical answer can, as I see it, be found in the recorded teaching of Jesus.

A few minutes before writing these words I happened to read a letter published in the *Church Times* deploring a leading article on 'Missiles and Morals'. On this article itself – or the harrowing moral debate to which it made a controversial contribution – I make no comment here. But the letter of protest, in taking exception to the 'assumption' that violence is 'the most effective power in deterring enemies', referred to three passages in the New Testament, two of them from the teaching of Jesus. I quote:

We were once told not to deter, still less destroy, our enemies, but to love them. Moreover, the folly of a strong man seeking to protect his goods in peace by such means was thoroughly exposed: a stronger man will inevitably come along sooner or later to undermine such false security.

But this sort of argument will not do. Jesus certainly taught that we must love our enemies – but not, surely, the system they may seek to impose? I am reminded of a Dutch student who, during the Nazi occupation of Holland, was asked if he had anything he wished to say before being sentenced to death for participation in the Resistance Movement. 'Yes', he replied, 'I want to say that I have no hatred whatever for the German people. But I detest the practices of their present Government and have been fighting against their imposition here. For this I am ready to die.' This is a perfectly valid distinction, for the Dutch had watched Jews being dragged away to extermination.

What, again, is the relevance, in the context of international armaments, of a reference to a strong man whose security would 'inevitably' be undermined, sooner or later, by one stronger than he? This metaphor was used by Jesus to illustrate the fact that it was only by his own advent and mission that Satan's captives could be freed. Surely the agonising issues of war or peace, resistance or enslavement – to say nothing of the teaching of Jesus *per se* – deserve better arguments, and more accurate exegesis, than this? Nor can Jesus' own example, pre-eminently in Gethsemane, be quoted as decisive in this context. To have organised resistance then would have been in self-defence rather than in that of others; and Jesus was well aware that what he was about to suffer was the very purpose for which he had come (John 12:27). I can find no *final* answer in the teaching of Jesus to the appalling problems that face us today – other than his Parousia.

One last point remains to be noted. People often speak as though the realisation of social justice – in any particular, sphere or community – represents an advance, however partial, in the establishment of the Kingdom of God on earth. But this tends to obscure the true meaning of that term as used in the teaching of Jesus.

As we have seen, the Kingdom he proclaimed had both a present and an eschatological meaning. In the latter sense, that Kingdom will be consummated only by the direct intervention of God, in salvation and in judgment, to establish his universal reign and to eliminate all evil, while in the former (or present) sense it has already come, in the person and mission of Jesus, as God's kingly rule in the hearts of those who give him their unqualified allegiance. It is certainly true that God commands social justice, so its realisation in any instance or degree is *per se* in accordance with his will; but it is impossible to speak of God's 'kingly rule' in regard to individuals or communities who ignore or defy his lordship, however much their behaviour may, in some particulars, conform to his design for his world.

Christians have a clear obligation to work for social and economic justice, to protest against evil, and to promote all that represents God's purposes for human life. This is an integral part of the mission on which he has sent them. But it is a misuse of terms, strictly speaking, to suggest that they are in this way 'building' or 'bringing in' the Kingdom. That can and will be done only by God himself when his hour strikes. In the meantime it is our duty to persuade men and women to submit to his kingly rule by our witness to the Gospel (as an essential part of the wider mission of succour, reconciliation and resistance to all injustice that he has entrusted to us) and to pray 'Amen; come, Lord Jesus' (Rev. 22:20).

Part III

The Consummation of the Kingdom

Chapter
7

The Person, Cross, Resurrection and Ascension of Jesus

The Person of Jesus: his explicit and implicit claims

In the preceding chapters of this book we have considered the teaching of Jesus about the Kingdom of God, eternal life and salvation (three concepts so closely inter-connected as to be almost synonymous); about the way in which he 'fulfilled' the Law and the Prophets; and about the canons of personal and social ethics appropriate to the Kingdom. In the course of this teaching it is recorded that Jesus referred to himself, or was addressed by others, by a number of different titles – Son of Man, Messiah, Son of God or simply 'the Son'. There has been much scholarly debate about each of these titles, and had my subject been Christology as such this would have demanded detailed discussion. But in a book about the teaching of Jesus as a whole, a brief and somewhat dogmatic summary must suffice.

In the New Testament the title 'the Son of Man' is found almost exclusively on the lips of Jesus himself; and the suggestion that it was first applied to him by the Church seems to be virtually devoid of evidence (cf. Moule, *Christology*, p. 20) and intrinsically most unlikely – since it would have been wholly inadequate to express their Easter faith. The phrase 'son of man' was often, it is true, used in Semitic idiom as no more than a synonym for man (e.g. Ps. 8:4; Ezek. 2:1; Dan. 8:17). But Moule has shown that in the Gospels the phrase used is almost invariably '*the* Son of Man' (*Christology*, pp. 13ff.) and Caird insists that, while there are a few places where it is due to editorial insertion,

> in general there is adequate evidence that it was Jesus' own
> choice of title, perhaps a deliberately mysterious and
> ambiguous one. It enabled him, without actually claiming to
> be Messiah, to indicate his essential unity with mankind, and
> above all with the weak and humble, and also his special
> function as predestined representative of the new Israel and
> bearer of God's judgment and Kingdom (*Luke*, p. 94.).

I am myself convinced that Barrett is right in his statement that
the Gospel use of the phrase 'rests primarily upon Daniel 7,
where the term makes its first appearance in an eschatological
context'[1] – a view which T. W. Manson and C. F. D. Moule
strongly support.[2] But I am totally unimpressed by the suggestion that Jesus (sometimes, at least) used the term to refer to
some specific individual other than himself, and I find no convincing evidence for this in the statement recorded in Mark
8:38: 'If anyone is ashamed of me and mine in this wicked and
godless age, the Son of Man will be ashamed of him, when he
comes in the glory of his Father and of the holy angels'. It seems
clear that in the Aramaic spoken by Jesus the expression was
used either for 'a man' in general or for 'one' in reference to the
speaker himself, and that Jesus frequently used the term as a
circumlocution for 'I' (sometimes with, and sometimes
without, its apocalyptic overtones); so why should he not have
spoken in Mark 8:38 of a man being 'ashamed of me' in
reference to his earthly life, and of 'the Son of Man' being
ashamed of that man in reference to his Parousia? Nor can I
accept Barrett's categorical statement that 'if Jesus did speak of
himself as Son of man [which Barrett seems to accept] it *cannot*
have been in such a way as to create the impression that the Son
of man was the Messiah' (*Gospel*, p. 33; my italics). On the
contrary, the juxtaposition of the two titles in the context of
Peter's confession (Mark 8:29, 31) and, still more, that of Jesus'
reply to the question put to him on oath at his trial by the High
Priest are, I believe, of more than redactional significance.
     It was this affirmation that precipitated Jesus' condemn-

ation by the Sanhedrin for 'blasphemy' – not in the narrow, technical sense, which involved actually pronouncing the divine name, but in the wider connotation of usurping the divine prerogatives. It is in this sense that the term seems to be normally used in the New Testament (cf. Mark 2:7, in the context of Jesus' saying to a paralysed man, 'My son, your sins are forgiven'; and John 10:31, where the Jews picked up stones to stone him for blasphemy, saying 'You, a mere man, claim to be God'). As Dodd put it:

> The evangelists, I conclude, John and the Synoptists alike, take the view that Jesus was charged with blasphemy because he spoke and acted in ways which implied that he stood in a special relation with God, so that his words carried divine authority and his actions were instinct with divine power. Unless this could be believed, the implied claim was an affront to the deepest religious sentiments of his people, a profanation of sanctities ... Whether or not Jesus had put himself forward as Messiah, the implied claim was messianic at least, perhaps rather messianic plus.[3]

While, therefore, it seems clear that in his public preaching Jesus did not claim to be Messiah (in part, presumably, because he did not understand his vocation in terms of his contemporaries' view of the person and mission of a messianic king as a national deliverer), the evidence that he accepted the title in private is very strong. His attitude is typified, I think, by his reply to Peter's confession of faith in the words: 'You did not learn that from mortal man; it was revealed to you by my heavenly Father'.

Moule, again, remarks that the triumphal entry (Mark 11) 'looks uncommonly like a deliberate messianic gesture or demonstration', and argues that the 'tenacity' with which the title 'Christ' was used by the Church even of a crucified Messiah 'is most plausibly explained if Jesus himself had accepted the royal title, but, during his ministry, had so radically reinterpreted it that it became natural to his followers to use it in this new way' (*Christology*, pp. 33f.). So he quotes with approval Cullmann's dictum that 'The early Church believed in Christ's messiahship only because it believed that Jesus believed himself to be the Messiah' (*Christology, p. 8*).

But the High Priest's question went farther than this, for Mark records his words as 'Are you the Messiah, the Son of the Blessed One?' To this Jesus replied: 'I am; and you will see the Son of Man seated on the right hand of God [literally, 'of the Power'] and coming with the clouds of heaven' (Mark 14:62f.). In Matthew's and Luke's accounts Jesus points out that the question was posed in the High Priest's own words; but his reply was, at least by implication, precisely the same, and Rudolf Otto argues strongly that this confession that he was both Messiah and Son of Man '*could* not have been invented by the church.'[4] The phrase 'the Son of the Blessed One' (i.e. God) on the High Priest's lips is usually taken as no more than a messianic title; but Cranfield insists that it seems improbable that 'Son of God' was in fact so used in pre-Christian Palestinian Judaism and that it is 'more likely that the words were added because the authorities were aware of some such saying of Jesus as Mt. 11:27 = Lk. 10:22 or had drawn conclusions from the parable of the Wicked Husbandmen' (*Mark*, p. 443).

The fact is that the explicit references to the Father/Son relationship between Jesus and his heavenly Father in John's Gospel are by no means wholly absent from the synoptic tradition. In Mark the most unequivocal such reference is Jesus' statement that the time of the Parousia was known to no one, 'not even the Son; only the Father' (13:32). The reference is also overt, as we have seen, in Matthew 11:27 and Luke 10:22. On the latter Caird comments:

> Many scholars have doubted whether Jesus could really have made the claims attributed to him in this passage. Hase described it as 'an aerolite from the Johannine heaven', the implication being that such a theological affirmation has no place in the more terrestrial narrative of the Synoptic Gospels ... Modern scholars would be a little more hesitant about the assumption that sayings found in John's Gospel

are necessarily unhistorical. If we find a 'Johannine' saying in Q, the oldest strand of the synoptic tradition, the natural inference is, not that Q is untrustworthy, but that John had access to a reliable sayings source ... Nor is the passage unique even in the Q tradition, for it contains little which is not at least implicit in the stories of the baptism and temptation of Jesus (*Luke*, p. 146).

It is implicit, too, in the way in which Jesus habitually addressed his prayers to 'Abba' ('my own Father'), and in the unique authority, inherent in both his teaching and his works of power, that so amazed his contemporaries (Mark 1:22, 27). We have seen how he is reported by Luke to have said, 'Until John, it was the Law and the Prophets: since then, there is the good news of the Kingdom of God and everyone is vigorously pressing forward into it' (Luke 16:16). With his advent a new age had dawned; he had 'fulfilled' the Law and the Prophets by personifying all that the prophets had predicted and by giving in his own authoritative teaching what the Mosaic law had adumbrated by precept, type and symbol. In place of the prophetic 'Thus saith the Lord' he had repeatedly introduced his teaching by the authoritative 'Amen, I say to you' – an introduction which, as Leslie Houlden aptly remarks, 'invites no discussion, uses no logically grounded persuasion. It simply commands obedience' (*Ethics*, p. 14).

It is also significant that, in Matthew 7:21-9, Jesus quietly – and without any sort of explanation – associates himself with the Day of Judgment in the unequivocal statement that

> When that day comes, many will say to me, 'Lord, Lord, did we not prophesy in your name, cast out devils in your name, and in your name perform many miracles?' Then I will tell them to their face, 'I never knew you: out of my sight, you and your wicked ways!'

The fundamental test was to be whether they had, or had not, heard and acted on 'these words of mine'. In much the same way, he claimed to have 'the right on earth to forgive sins' (Mark 2:10), to be 'Lord of the Sabbath' (Matt. 12:8), to be the only way to the Father (Matt. 11:27) and to have 'full authority in heaven and on earth' (Matt. 28:18).

It is equally significant that it is in John's Gospel, which puts such unequivocal emphasis on his deity, that Jesus repeatedly emphasises his complete dependence on, and obedience to, the Father. Reference has already been made (p. 96 above) to what C. H. Dodd has termed 'the parable of the Apprentice' in John 5:19f.; but the same refrain comes again and again: 'the teaching that I give is not my own; it is the teaching of him who sent me' (John 7:16); 'I do nothing on my own authority, but in all that I say, I have been taught by my Father' (John 8:28); 'I do not speak on my own authority, but the Father who sent me has himself commanded me what to say and how to speak. I know that his commands are eternal life. What the Father has said to me, therefore, that is what I speak' (John 12:49f.); 'I am not myself the source of the words I speak to you: it is the Father who dwells in me doing his own work' (John 14:10). This is the secret that explains how the Jesus of the Gospels, although not omniscient,[5] could teach with such absolute authority.

When, it may be asked, did he first become aware of his unique relationship to his heavenly Father? Any attempt to probe the self-consciousness of Jesus must inevitably be speculative, but I believe Louis Bouyer is right when he insists that 'We must not try to represent to ourselves this consciousness of Jesus, whether messianic or filial, as being essentially, and still less as being primarily, a reflex consciousness of its own identity'. Instead, we should

recognize that this consciousness of Jesus, like every normal consciousness, was the consciousness of an object before becoming a consciousness of its own subject. The consciousness of Jesus, as the human consciousness of the Son of God, was before all else consciousness *of God*. Jesus was 'the Christ, the Son of the living God', not directly by knowing that he was, but because he knew God *as the Father* . . . What is unique in the consciousness of Jesus of Nazareth is that it was pierced and traversed, from its first awakening, by that intuition, which was to precede, penetrate, and saturate all his states of consciousness, whatever they might be (*Le Fils*, p. 510).

Very similarly, Galot regards the Aramaic word *Abba*, 'the familiar term that Jewish children used to talk to their father' (which, he believes, Jesus habitually used in place of the more formal terms in which Jews were wont to address the transcendent Father in heaven), as the key to Jesus' self-consciousness. 'Human beings', he affirms, 'do not first of all exist in their separate self-enclosures, to enter later on into relation with others ... An "ego" [*moi*] has meaning only in its relation with other "egos".' So he insists that 'Abba'

is the most apt term to indicate to us how the consciousness of divine sonship was formed in Jesus ... No other term could have been as meaningful to witness to the point at which the consciousness of divine sonship is, in Jesus, a consciousness that is perfectly human. *Abba* is the term used by someone who has a consciousness like that of other children, but with this difference, that in this case the father is not a human father, but is God (*La Personne*, pp. 155, 162).

We meet the first indication of Jesus' consciousness of this relationship in the reply he is recorded as giving to Mary's gentle reproach when, at the age of twelve, he stayed behind in the Temple: 'Did you not know that I was bound to be in my Father's house?' (Luke 2:49). Testimony also comes from the accounts of his baptism and temptation, for Caird persuasively argues that these *must* represent the teaching that Jesus himself gave to his disciples, since

the pious ingenuity of the early Church could no more have created these stories than the parables of the Good Samaritan and the Prodigal Son ... The voice from heaven addressed Jesus in a composite quotation from scripture (Ps. 2:7; Isa. 42:1). Psalm 2 proclaims the accession of the anointed king, who is to rule the nations with a rod of iron. Isa. 42:1-6 is the first of a series of prophecies about the Servant of the Lord, who has been chosen to carry true religion to the Gentiles and who, in achieving this mission, must suffer indignity, rejection and death. Thus the words which he had heard must have meant to Jesus that he was being designated to both these offices, *anointed ... with the Holy Spirit and with power* (Acts 10:37; cf. Luke 4:18), sent out to establish the reign of God, not with the iron sceptre but with patient and self-forgetful service. Remembering Luke's story of the boy Jesus, we cannot suppose that all this now flashed upon him as a new and startling revelation ... The baptism experience represented the end of a long development, of deepening appreciation of the divine fatherhood and his own filial responsibility, of growing insight into his mission and the world's need, of meditation on the meaning of the scriptures and their application to himself (Caird, *Luke*, pp. 76f.; Matt. 3:17; Mark 1:11; Luke 3:22).

In the temptation, on the other hand, it was not God's voice saying, 'You are my Son', but another voice saying, 'If [in the sense, probably, of 'since'] you are the Son of God ... ' that he heard. So he had to decide where this voice came from, and whether the suggestions of how 'the Son of God' should act were valid. And he decided that the voice which prompted him to take these actions was not that of God, but of the devil (cf. Matt. 4:1-10; Mark 1:12f.; Luke 4:1-13).

It is also noteworthy in this context that Galot, who shows himself well acquainted with the vast literature on the significance of the Son of Man sayings, insists that Jesus identified himself with that mysterious figure, and that he not only fulfilled but transcended the prophetic expectations. But, he continues, while 'the way in which Jesus speaks of himself in the third person by describing himself as the Son of Man is strange and exceptional, the way in which he speaks of himself as "I" is no less so'. He then argues that the *Ego eimi* ('I am') passages imply both a divine status and also a filial relationship to the heavenly Father (*La Personne*, pp. 82f.).

From all this it appears that the much longer discourses about his relationship with the Father recorded in John's Gospel do not really break any essentially new ground. Allowance must, no doubt, be made for the fact that the fourth Evangelist (or 'the Beloved Disciple' whose testimony underlies the Gospel) has spelt out the meaning of what Jesus taught on this subject in the terms in which he had come to understand it. It is, in fact, often impossible to draw any hard and fast line between the words he attributes to Jesus himself and his own reflections upon them. At times, Jesus is recorded in this Gospel as making statements that sound uncharacteristically harsh – as is also the case in the synoptic Gospels when Jesus was confronting religious hypocrisy. But Tasker has justly remarked that

> there is no valid reason for supposing that, when dealing with the Rabbis in Jerusalem, He did not debate with them in rabbinic fashion the nature of His claims; and it may well be just this side of the Lord's ministry that the Galilean disciples knew little about, but with which the fourth Evangelist was more familiar, particularly if ... he was himself a Jerusalem disciple (*John*, pp. 30f.).

In sum, it is clear that Jesus, as God-in-manhood, lived – as every man *should* always live – in utter dependence on, glad obedience to, and continual fellowship with, his heavenly Father. It is precisely for this reason that, although any suggestion that the Evangelists depict him as walking about saying 'I am God' is a gross caricature, he certainly did at times speak and act in a way appropriate to God alone.

He came proclaiming the advent of the Kingdom of God, for example, and we have seen that, in the present, this meant the kingly rule of God in the hearts of those who respond to his summons, and will, in the future, mean the universal consummation of that rule, both in salvation and in judgment. The only way to enter that Kingdom, here and now, is by allegiance to Jesus, and the coming Kingdom will be his as well as God's (cf. Matt. 16:28; Luke 22:29f.). Thus in some of Jesus' parables 'the King' represents the Father (cf. Matt. 18:23, 35; 22:2-14) and in others Jesus himself (cf. Luke 19:12; Matt. 25:31-46). It is he whose very name means Saviour,[6] and to whom all judgment will be given (John 5:22, 27); and the eternal throne will be that 'of God and of the Lamb' (Rev. 22:3). In Cranfield's words we can

> actually go so far as to say that the Kingdom of God *is* Jesus and that he *is* the Kingdom ... He is himself the fulfilment of God's promises, God's royal intervention in judgment and mercy. The fact that the Kingdom of God is, for the evangelists, identical with Jesus himself is indicated by the way in which a reference to Jesus may be parallel to a reference to the Kingdom (*Mark*, p.66).

And precisely the same can be said of both eternal life and salvation.

His teaching about the Cross

My recent reference to 'the throne of God and of the Lamb' may serve to remind us that it was immediately after Peter's confession at Caesarea Philippi of Jesus as the Messiah that we are told that Jesus began to teach his disciples that 'the Son of Man must suffer' (Mark 8:29-31). This was quite incomprehensible to men whose concept of the Messiah was the very reverse of a Suffering Servant; and Peter went so far as to take Jesus on one side and start to rebuke him, saying: 'Heaven forbid! No, Lord, this shall never happen to you!' (Matt. 16:22). But this was a repetition of the persistent temptation that had come to Jesus in the desert to take a short cut rather than fulfil the agonising destiny to which he was ever more firmly setting his face, and it earned Peter the exceedingly sharp rebuke: 'Away with you, Satan; you are a stumbling block to me. You think as men think, not as God thinks' (Matt. 16:23).

This must have come as a bewildering shock to the man to

whom Jesus had just said:

> Simon son of Jonah, you are favoured indeed! You did not learn that from any mortal man; it was revealed to you by my heavenly Father. And I say this to you: You are Peter, the Rock; and on this rock I will build my church, and the forces of death [or 'the gates of Hades'] shall never overpower it. I will give you the keys of the kingdom of Heaven; what you forbid [or 'bind'] on earth shall be forbidden [or 'bound'] in heaven, and what you allow ['loose'] on earth shall be allowed ['loosed'] in heaven (Matt. 16:17ff.).

And it was indeed given to Peter to open the door of the Kingdom both to Jews and to Gentiles – by his proclamation of the Gospel on the day of Pentecost and in the house of Cornelius, respectively (Acts 2:14-41; 10:34-48); and to exercise discipline in the infant Church (Acts 5:1-11).

A very similar commission was also given to all those in the Upper Room on the first Easter Day (John 20:19-23). But three points need to be noted. First, the use of these 'keys' to open and shut the Kingdom, to forgive sins or to 'retain' them, was no discretionary right but one that fundamentally consisted in proclaiming with authority the conditions on which God himself promises forgiveness or pronounces judgment. A vivid example of this can be found in the commission given to Jeremiah when God said: 'Now, I have put my words in your mouth. See, today I appoint you over nations and kingdoms to uproot and tear down, to destroy and overthrow, to build and to plant' (Jer. 1:9f.) – for all this was done by God himself, not by his mouthpiece, Jeremiah. Secondly, it is vital to remember that it was only by Jesus' treading the path to the Cross that the door to the Kingdom could be opened and the message of free forgiveness proclaimed. Thirdly, as the fourth ARCIC Report makes clear, there is no biblical evidence for Peter's priority being passed on to successive Bishops of Rome.

After this first prediction of suffering a number of similar, but considerably more detailed, predictions are recorded in the Gospels (cf. Mark 10:33f.). Many scholars deny the authenticity of all these sayings, which they dismiss as *vaticinia ex eventu*, while others insist that the growing hostility of the Jewish leaders was quite enough, in the light of Old Testament history, to give Jesus a strong presentiment of impending doom.[7] But the Evangelists consistently report these predictions in terms not of probability but of necessity; and Barrett cogently argues that if Jesus had simply come to realise that his present course would inevitably precipitate a violent end to his ministry, he would presumably have changed his tactics. So he concludes that, if Jesus was able to predict his death, 'and there is no reason why he should not have done so', he must have interpreted it 'in the same eschatological context in which he interpreted his ministry as a whole' (*Gospel*, p.38).

It is when it comes to this matter of interpretation that I find the arguments of scholars such as Barrett and Morna Hooker so unconvincing. Barrett is perfectly right in observing that the Gospels tell us that Jesus did not actually say that the 'Messiah' had to suffer, but that 'the Son of Man must suffer'. But he concedes that this term, at least in the context of these predictions, was used by Jesus in reference to himself; and the evidence that Jesus knew himself to be the Messiah (in the sense in which he understood that term) seems to me overwhelmingly strong. The reason why he did not make this claim in his *public* ministry, and why he preferred the title 'Son of Man' even in the context of Peter's messianic confession, is not far to seek (cf. pp. 37, 153 above), since any such reference to 'Messiah' would have given rise to expectations and implications that he did not himself share; whereas the argument that Jesus did not think of himself in terms of the 'Servant' passages in Isaiah, and still less as a 'suffering servant', seems to me laboured and unconvincing.

That the early Church turned to Isaiah 53 to throw light on the meaning of Christ's death on the Cross seems to be conclusively proved by 1 Peter 2:21-5. In regard to this quotation Morna Hooker concedes that there is 'a blending of phrases from Deutero-Isaiah with the historical events of Christ's Passion: these events are not distorted to agree with Isa. 53, but are interpreted in the light of that chapter' (*Servant*,

p. 125). It seems to me particularly significant that the writer began this allusion to the Passion as an example of patience in suffering which Christians ought to emulate. But he evidently felt that he could not leave the reference there, and *must* (even out of context) emphasise the atoning efficacy of that death by specifically stating that 'in his own person he carried our sins to the gallows', and that 'by his wounds you have been healed'.

True, the two passages in the synoptic Gospels in which Isaiah 53 is unmistakably quoted (Matt. 8:17 and Luke 22:37) do not carry this significance in any explicit way. Matthew seems to have quoted from the Hebrew rather than the Septuagint, and so to have taken the words in the literal sense of the cure of physical sickness through the healing ministry of Jesus, rather than spiritualising the passage as a reference to sins – which is, surely, the primary meaning of Isaiah 53, if verse 4 is to be taken together with verse 3. But I think David Hill is right when he concludes that, 'unless Matthew is quoting a verse which had already become detached from its literary context and from Old Testament theology, it seems unlikely that the idea of substitution and the vicarious action of the Servant is entirely absent here' (*Matthew*, p. 161).

In Luke the quotation from Isaiah 53 is reported from the lips of Jesus himself, and the meaning seems to be that 'the reason why the disciples must be ready for the worst is that their Master also faces the worst' (Marshall, *Luke*, p. 525). But in our context the significance of this quotation is, surely, that at this climactic moment the mind of Jesus turned instinctively to Isaiah 53; that he applied the quotation to himself; and that he insisted that it *must* be fulfilled. The statement that he, innocent as he was, would be 'numbered with the transgressors' is at least consonant with vicarious suffering; and it seems exceedingly unlikely that the very next sentence in Isaiah 53 ('For he bore the sin of many, and made intercession for the transgressors') was not also in his mind, although his recorded quotation stopped short at the reference to a danger in which his disciples would have a share. This logion, with its startling (if metaphorical) injunction that his disciples should buy a sword, would certainly seem to be authentic, and to provide positive evidence that Jesus – in spite of recent denials – did in fact identify himself with the Suffering Servant of Jahweh.

When we turn to Mark 10:45, Hooker and Barrett are no doubt right in maintaining that the verse *could* be explained without reference to the Servant Songs in general or Isaiah 53 in particular;[8] but it seems to me that the evidence points much more decisively in the opposite direction.[9] As in the case of 1 Peter 2:21ff., the immediate context of the words 'For even the Son of Man did not come to be served but to serve, and to surrender his life as a ransom for many' (Mark 10:45; cf. Matt. 20:38) is that of example rather than atonement; but I can see nothing strange in the fact that Jesus is reported in the final clause as going on to reinforce his example of leadership characterised by humble service by a reference to the redeeming death which would constitute his supreme act of self-sacrifice for others. The parallels between this saying and Isaiah 53 are not only in what R. T. France terms 'verbal echoes' but in 'the underlying thought'[10] – although Barrett's categorical statement that the logion 'contains no direct literary allusion to Isaiah 53' (*Gospel*, p. 40) seems much too strong.

The authenticity of Mark 14:24 (Matt. 26:28; Luke 22:20) is very seldom questioned, but Barrett (*Gospel*, p. 40) insists that 'any contact between Mark 14:24 and Isaiah 53 is even more remote'. On the surface this is certainly true, since the primary reference is clearly to the covenant concluded at Sinai (Ex. 24:3-11) and to the 'new covenant' promised in Jeremiah 31:31ff. The Sinaitic covenant was based on the redemptive act of the exodus from Egypt, was sealed by the blood of animal sacrifice and coupled with the moral demands epitomised in the Decalogue; whereas the new covenant was to be founded on the redemptive act of Jesus' 'exodus' (cf. Luke 9:31), to be sealed by his own blood and to substitute a law written on men's hearts and minds for commandments engraved on tablets of stone, which challenged their unwilling, and even impossible, obedience.

Yet it remains true that the Servant is referred to, in both Isaiah 42:6 and 49:8, as a 'covenant' to the people; that the words 'poured out *for many*' are distinctly reminiscent of Isaiah 53:12; and that 'the whole idea of "dying on behalf of", which is central to Mark 14:24, renders an allusion to the Servant virtually certain' (France, *Jesus*, p. 122 cf. Cullmann, *Christology*, p. 64).[11]

After referring to Isaiah 42:6 and 49:8 (in which 'God makes his Servant "a *berīt* [covenant] for the people" '), G. Dalman points out that Isaiah 53:10 and 12 make it clear that 'in order to be this he will have to pass through death', and adds: 'In the whole of the O.T. here alone is it to be found that there is a relationship between the *berīt* of God and the death of its Mediator' (*Jesus-Jeshua*, p. 170). Nor is the evidence provided by the Last Supper by any means confined to this single verse.[12]

Several other allusions by Jesus to his coming death are reported in the Gospels, of which two examples must suffice. All four Evangelists record his reference in Gethsemane to the 'cup' of suffering that he was to accept from his Father's hand, and the three Synoptists refer to this also as a 'baptism' that he knew he must undergo. Luke tells us that the risen Christ explained, from 'every part of the Scriptures', why it was essential that the Messiah should suffer (Luke 24:25ff., 44ff.). This was teaching that the disciples could never really understand until, after the event, the Holy Spirit revealed its meaning (cf. John 16:12f.). Naturally enough, it assumed a major significance in the apostolic preaching (cf. Acts and the Pauline epistles).

It is particularly interesting to note that the writer of the Epistle to the Hebrews sums up the significance of Jesus' atoning death by his categorical statement that 'it is impossible for the blood of bulls and goats to take away sins', and then quotes the prophetic utterance of Psalm 40:6-8 (Septuagint version) as a prediction of the fact that animal sacrifices were to be replaced, in the fullness of time, by that rational, voluntary and final sacrifice to which the Levitical sacrifices had all pointed forward (cf. Heb. 10:1-18). This sacrifice, he says, was an essential part of the purpose of God in the Incarnation, and it was to this that Jesus dedicated himself in supremely costly, and efficacious, obedience.[13]

His Teaching about his Resurrection and Ascension

In the majority of Jesus' predictions of his death he is also
reported as saying that he would 'rise again after three days' (cf.
Mark 8:31). As has often been remarked, if this prediction had
been merely attributed to him by the Church after the event,
the wording would in all probability have been 'on the third
day' – as in the apostolic preaching. John also records that
Jesus once said to his critics 'Destroy this temple, and in three
days I will raise it again' (John 2:19); a statement which Mark
reports as being quoted against him, in its literal sense, at his
trial before the Sanhedrin (Mark 14:57f.) But during the days
of his ministry his disciples were quite unable to understand
that the one they believed to be the Messiah would really die a
violent death; so any reference to the Resurrection fell on deaf
ears. It was only after the event that they came to understand
this metaphorical reference to the 'temple' (cf. John 2:21f.) or
his other, much more explicit, statements about what was to
happen to him; and it was only then that he could 'open their
minds' to understand the prophetic predictions of the necessity
for, and meaning of, his passion and the allusions to his life
beyond the grave. In such an exposition Isaiah 53 would almost
inevitably have assumed a major importance (cf. not only
verses 3-10(a), but also verses 10(b)-12).

Luke records that the risen Lord told the two disciples on the
road to Emmaus that the Messiah had to suffer 'before entering
upon his glory' (Luke 24:26). In the context this last phrase
must mean his resurrection, ascension and 'exaltation'. But the
life, death and resurrection of Jesus were all of a piece; and
'glory' is a word that can appropriately be attributed to him in a
number of different ways. John, for example, records that his
disciples had (at least by hindsight) 'seen in him', throughout
his earthly life, 'such glory as befits the Father's only Son, full
of grace and truth' (John 1:14, 2:11). Again, when Judas left the
Paschal Supper to betray him, John reports that Jesus said:
'Now the Son of Man is glorified, and in him God is glorified. If
God is glorified in him, God will also glorify him in himself;
and he will glorify him now' (John 13:31f.) – for his

humiliation and agony on the Cross, and what he accomplished there, were not only the reason for his subsequent exaltation but an essential element in his glory.

Thus John saw no contradiction in the phrases he records in Jesus' 'High Priestly' prayer:

> Father, the time has come. Glorify your Son, that your Son may glorify you ... I have brought you glory on earth by completing the work you gave me to do. And now, Father, glorify me in your presence with the glory I had with you before the world began ... Father, I want those you have given me to be with me where I am, and to see my glory, the glory you have given me because you loved me before the creation of the world (John 17:1, 5, 24).

In the synoptic tradition, on the other hand, the logia about glory are almost all concerned with the Parousia, to which we shall turn in my next chapter.

There are very few sayings in the Gospels in which Jesus is reported as having spoken of his ascension as an event distinct from his exaltation. In John's Gospel he spoke of his return to the Father when he said: 'I am going away, and coming back to you. If you loved me you would have been glad to hear that I was going to the Father; for the Father is greater than I' (John 14:28) – for even in the unity of the triune Godhead there is a sense in which the eternal Son, who fully shares the divine nature (John 10:30), never questions the priority of the Father. Other sayings in which Jesus refers to 'going to the Father' can be found in John 14:12, 16:10 and 16:28. The only verse in which he speaks of his ascension as such in this Gospel is John 20:17, where the risen Lord says to Mary, 'Do not cling to me, for I am not yet ascended to the Father'. Somewhat similarly, what we call the 'Ascension' is referred to (although not described) in the synoptic Gospels only in Luke 24:50, which simply states that Jesus led his disciples out 'as far as Bethany, and blessed them with uplifted hands; and in the act of blessing he parted from them'. It is in Acts 1:9-11 that his visible withdrawal at the end of the forty days is described; and it is to this that the brief reference in Luke 24:50 almost certainly refers – for there is no valid reason to think that Luke intended his readers to imagine that all the events recorded in chapter 24 actually happened on Easter Day.

That said, I am myself convinced that we should look at the 'ascension' from two points of view: that of the risen Lord himself, and that of his disciples. From his point of view (and therefore that of eternal reality) I believe that he 'returned to the Father' on Easter Day, possibly after his interview with Mary. Then, during the forty days, he 'showed himself to his disciples' – whether singly or in groups – on a number of different occasions in his risen body (for the Resurrection was much more than the resuscitation of a corpse). During this period he 'gave ample proof that he was alive', and taught them much about himself and the Kingdom (cf. Luke 24 and Acts 1). Finally, when the forty days had come to an end, 'he was taken up before their very eyes' (Acts 1:9) on what we call Ascension Day – which was both a historical and a symbolical event. Historical, because I believe, with Michael Ramsey (*Resurrection*, pp. 121f.), that it is a record of something that actually happened; and symbolical, because it signified that the appearances of the forty days were over (for even Paul's vision on the road to Damascus was essentially different from these, as his own phraseology in 1 Corinthians 15:8 seems to imply).

Even during his earthly life, as we have seen, Jesus had spoken of his impending suffering and death, to be followed by his resurrection – although his disciples totally failed, at the time, to understand. He had also warned them that he would have to go away from them; but he had promised that he 'would not leave them bereft', for he would 'come back to them' (John 14:18f.). In the context this promise clearly referred to his return to their hearts in and through the Holy Spirit. But he had also told them that he was going 'to prepare a place for you', and that he would 'come back and receive you to myself' (John 14:2f.). So in my last chapter it is to this two-fold return, in the Holy Spirit and in the Parousia – together with the intervening mission of the Church – that we must turn.

Chapter
8

The Holy Spirit, the Mission of the Church and the Parousia

The Holy Spirit

Before his ascension the risen Christ is reported specifically to have told his disciples that their task was to be witnesses to him (Matt. 28:19; Luke 24:47f.; John 15:27; Acts 1:8). He instructed them, therefore, to stay in Jerusalem until he sent them 'the Father's promised gift' to 'clothe' or 'arm' them 'with power from on high' (Luke 24:49). Nor would this gift consist in a mere influence or power, but rather in one whom he referred to as 'another to be your Counsellor [Advocate, Comforter, Helper] ... the Spirit of truth' (John 14:26).

There are in fact singularly few references to the Holy Spirit in the teaching of Jesus recorded in the synoptic Gospels – a fact which points strongly to the conclusion that the synoptic tradition represents a faithful reflection of the teaching that Jesus himself actually gave, rather than of the experiences and concerns of the post-resurrection Church, in which the activity of the Holy Spirit was a matter of central concern. All the Synoptists, however, record his stern statement about 'slandering' or 'blaspheming against' the Holy Spirit (Mark 3:28f.; Matt. 12:31f.; Luke 12:10). In Matthew and Mark this saying is reported in the context of the allegation that it was 'only by Beelzebub, prince of the devils' – rather than by the Spirit or 'finger' of God (Matt. 12:28; Luke 11:20) – that Jesus himself drove out demons, whereas in Luke it comes in a somewhat different context.

All three Synoptists state that this sort of blasphemy constitutes a sin that is 'eternal' or 'beyond forgiveness', while

Matthew and Luke record that Jesus went on to say that 'Any man who speaks a word against the Son of Man will be forgiven; but if anyone speaks against the Holy Spirit, for him there is no forgiveness' (Matt. 12:32; cf. Luke 12:10). From the context in which this logion about slandering the Holy Spirit is recorded in Matthew and Mark it seems clear that the distinction intended is between opposition to Jesus and his teaching in general, on the one hand, and a deliberate attribution of his deeds and words to Satan, rather than to the Spirit of God, on the other. In Luke this same statement, which Jesus may well have made more than once, is placed in the context of acknowledging or denying him before men, and the promise that 'When you are brought before synagogues and state authorities, do not begin worrying about how you will conduct your defence or what you will say. For when the time comes the Holy Spirit will instruct you what to say' (Luke 12:8-12; cf. Matt. 10:19f.; Mark 13:11).

Elsewhere Luke records that Jesus said; 'Is there a father among you who will offer his son a snake when he asks for fish, or a scorpion when he asks for an egg? If you, then, bad [parents] as you are, know how to give your children what is good for them, how much more will the heavenly Father give the Holy Spirit to those who ask him!' (Luke 11:11ff.). In the same context Matthew reports that Jesus said: 'How much more will your heavenly Father give good things to those who ask him' (Matt. 7:11) – to which some MSS of Luke assimilate 'the Holy Spirit' in Luke 11:13. It is impossible to be sure what Jesus actually said. Did he say 'good things' (almost certainly in a spiritual sense) and Luke pick out the Holy Spirit as the summary or best of them all? Did Matthew expand or generalise an original reference to the supreme spiritual gift? Or did Jesus himself perhaps say both – whether adding the more comprehensive term to widen out the specific or adding the specific to put a special emphasis on what was supremely important?

For the rest, the only references in the synoptic Gospels to the Holy Spirit in the *teaching* of Jesus are, I think, confined to three contexts. First, a passing reference to the way in which the Spirit inspired the Old Testament writers, when he is reported as saying 'David himself, speaking by the Holy Spirit, declared: "The Lord said to my Lord: Sit at my right hand, until I put your enemies under your feet".' (Mark 12:36; cf. Matt. 22:43). Second, Luke's brief reference to the promise that the disciples would be 'clothed with power from on high' (Luke 24:49), which is explained in Acts 1:7 in the words 'But you will receive power when the Holy Spirit comes upon you'. Lastly, there is Matthew's trinitarian formula in the command to the disciples to 'baptize men everywhere in the name of the Father and the Son and the Holy Spirit' (Matt. 28:19).

There can be little or no doubt that this provides dominical authority for Christian baptism – and without such authority it is most unlikely that baptism would have been regularly practised in the Church from the very first. It seems probable, however, that the earliest baptismal *formula* was 'in the name of Jesus' (Acts 2:38; 8:16); and most scholars agree that it was only at a rather later date that baptism came to be administered in the name of the Trinity. In his comment on Matthew 28:19 Robin Nixon remarks that 'The reference to the Trinity here may not be intended as a baptismal formula but as a theological description of the meaning of the sacrament' (Nixon, *Matthew*, p. 850). But Donald Guthrie pertinently reminds us not only of the close connection in Acts between baptism and an experience of the Holy Spirit, but also of the link between the words 'and teach them to observe all that I have commanded you' (reported by Matthew in this immediate context) and Jesus' promise in John 14:26 that the Holy Spirit would 'call to mind all that I have told you' (*N. T. Theology*, pp. 526f.). So it is to the teaching of Jesus on this subject recorded in the fourth Gospel that we must now turn.

In the earlier part of that Gospel Jesus is reported as referring to the Holy Spirit little more than the Synoptists record. The major addition comes in the conversation with Nicodemus in chapter 3, where verse 5 should almost certainly be rendered 'Amen, amen, I tell you, unless a man is born of water and the Spirit, he cannot enter the Kingdom of God'. To spell Spirit here without a capital (as in the N.E.B.) makes the

following verses almost unintelligible, for surely the contrast in
verse 6 is between being born physically of human parents and
born spiritually of the Holy Spirit. The reference in verse 8 to
the fact that 'The wind blows where it wills; you hear the sound
of it, but you do not know where it comes from, or where it is
going. So with everyone who is born of the Spirit' is
particularly apt – not only because 'wind' and 'spirit' represent
the same word (*pneuma*) in Greek; but primarily because,
although the Holy Spirit cannot himself be seen, nor the
beginning or end of his work predicted, yet the effects of his
presence can be both seen and 'heard'.

It seems to me that John 6:63 should be read in the same way,
which would be brought out in a paraphrase like this: 'It is the
Spirit of God who gives life, human nature cannot do this. The
words that I have spoken to you are instinct with God's life-
giving Spirit'. It is distinctly possible that the word 'spirit'
should also be accorded a capital in the words recorded in
Jesus' talk with the Samaritan woman: 'God is spirit; and those
who worship him must worship in spirit and truth' (John 4:24).
This possibility is strengthened by the close association of the
Spirit with 'truth' and by the fact that the Evangelist interprets
Jesus' statement in John 7:37f. ('If a man is thirsty, let him
come to me and drink. Whoever believes in me, as the Scripture
has said, streams of living water will flow from within him') in
terms of 'the Spirit, whom those who believed in him were later
to receive'.

In this same context John throws light on the reason why
Jesus referred so seldom to the Spirit – in his public ministry, at
least – when he adds the words: 'Up to that time the Spirit had
not been given, since Jesus had not yet been glorified'. In this
Gospel, as we have noted, the focal point of Jesus'
'glorification' is his humiliation on the Cross; but we must never
separate the Cross from the empty tomb, and it was the risen
Lord who said to his disciples: 'Peace be with you! As the
Father sent me, I am sending you'. He then breathed on them,
saying 'receive the Holy Spirit' (John 20:21f.).

There has been much debate about the relationship between
this recorded episode and the full realisation of the Spirit's

presence and power for which, Luke tells us, they were told to wait in Jerusalem until the day of Pentecost (Acts 2). Many suggestions have been made. Thus C. K. Barrett, in his comments on this passage, writes: 'That John intended to depict an event of significance parallel to that of the first creation of man cannot be doubted; this was the beginning of the new creation'. Then with his usual historical, as distinct from theological, scepticism, he asserts:

> It does not seem possible to harmonize this account of a special bestowing of the Spirit with that contained in Acts 2; after this event there could be no more 'waiting' (Luke 24:48f.; Acts 1:4f.); the church could not be more fully equipped for its mission. The existence of divergent traditions of the constitutive gift of the Spirit is not surprising; it is probable that to the first Christians the resurrection of Jesus and his appearances to them, his exaltation (however that was understood), and the gift of the Spirit, appeared as one experience, which only later came to be described in separate elements and incidents (Barrett, *John*, p. 570).

But why need we indulge in such unwarranted speculation? The evidence for the empty tomb, the resurrection appearances and the termination of the 'forty days' – and, indeed, for the Pentecostal experience[1] – is very strong; and are there not many examples of receiving a gift on one occasion and coming into the realised possession and enjoyment of it somewhat later? Is not this, in fact, our common (although not invariable) experience in the Christian life? We turn to Christ and accept by faith his gift of forgiveness and regeneration; but the 'inward witness' of the Spirit's presence and power may be instantaneous or delayed, 'sudden' or progressive. I can see no reason why we should be forced to choose, in this matter, between John 20 and Acts 2.

It is in the 'Farewell Discourses', to which John 13:31-16:33 are devoted, that the most important teaching about the Holy Spirit reported in the Gospels is to be found. As we have seen, it

is recorded that Jesus promised his disciples that, when he went
back to the Father, 'I will not leave you bereft; I am coming
back to you' (14:19) in the form of the 'Spirit-Paraclete', who
'will teach you everything, and will call to mind all that I have
told you' (14:26). This 'other Counsellor' would not 'speak on
his own authority' (16:13), but would 'bear witness to me' and
enable them to do the same (15:26f.; Acts 1:8). It would, indeed
be 'for [their] good' that he himself should 'go away', because
only so could he send this Counsellor (16:5ff.), 'who would
convict ['convince', 'confute'] the world about sin and
righteousness and judgment' (16:8), and guide the disciples into
all truth' (16:13).

These passages are explicit about the functions of the Holy
Spirit. But they also make it very clear that, although the Greek
word *pneuma* is neuter, the Spirit as the 'other Counsellor' is as
personal as the one he was to represent. The fact that we are
told that he 'proceeds' ['issues', 'emanates', 'goes out'] from the
Father, in a way which is comparable with, although not
identical to, the way in which the Son was eternally 'begotten'
by the Father, shows that he, too, shares the divine nature.

What, then, of the controversial *filioque* clause – the addition
to the early credal statement to which the Orthodox Church
raises such strong objections – that the Spirit proceeds 'from
the Father and the Son'? In these passages Jesus is in fact
recorded as saying in John 14:16 that 'I will ask the Father, and
he will give you another to be your Counsellor'; in 14:26 that
'the Father will send [him] in my name'; in 15:26 that 'I will
send to you from the Father the Spirit of truth who proceeds
from the Father'; and in 16:7 that 'I will send him to you'. So on
the vexed question of how, precisely, these somewhat varied
statements are to be construed, I shall venture to make only
two comments. First, that these verses not only emphasise, yet
again, the essential unity of the Father and the Son, but also
represent a distinct, if inchoate, trinitarian formulation.
Second, that it seems to me that the compromise wording
which has often been proposed, 'who proceeds from the Father
through the Son', would satisfy all the available evidence: that
the Father is consistently accorded the 'priority' (not in the

sense of time, but as fount and origin of the Godhead), since it was by him that the Son was eternally 'begotten', and it is from him that the Spirit eternally 'proceeds'; but that, in his ministry to the Church, the Spirit was 'sent' by the Father at the request and in the name of the Son, who can also be said to have 'sent' him to be his *alter ego*. The ultimate emphasis is, therefore, on the unity of the triune God.

Another question is how we are to regard these 'Farewell Discourses' in the fourth Gospel and the High Priestly Prayer that follows. This is the most extreme example of the point discussed briefly in the first chapter of this book: namely, whether the statements attributed to Jesus in the Gospels can be regarded in a very real sense as his *ipsissima vox*, although not, in very many cases, as his *ipsissima verba* (in translation) – or even, on occasion, as the *ipsissimus sensus* of some specific logia. Put in other words, can we accept them as a fair, reliable and authoritative reflection of what he actually taught and what that teaching means, although they are clearly not a complete, chronological or verbatim record?

To affirm, as many do, that these chapters, in particular, represent no more than a 'reading back' into the record of the life of Jesus of the subsequent experiences of the apostolic Church, and of the musings of this Evangelist, is to me quite unacceptable – although this is not to suggest that they represent precise reportage of teaching which was all necessarily given on the same occasion. But Guthrie aptly observes that 'the extraordinary activity of the Spirit at Pentecost and after' would have been left 'without adequate explanation, if Jesus had not prepared the disciples in the manner that John's narrative supposes' in his last, confidential talks with them. Thus 'it may not unjustly be claimed that the Paraclete sayings in John provide a key for the right understanding of the Spirit's activities in Acts' (*N. T. Theology*, pp. 529f.) – and, it may be said, an outstanding example of three of the functions that he was to fulfil: to bring the teaching of Jesus back to his disciples' memory (or from their subconscious to their conscious minds); to enlighten them as to its meaning in a way that, at the time when it was given, they were unable to understand or even 'bear'; and to 'guide [them] into all the truth' (14:26; 16:12f.).

The Church's Mission

It is in the context of the promise of the Holy Spirit that we read in Acts 1:4-11 that the risen Lord explicitly told his disciples that they were not to indulge in idle speculations 'about dates or times' – or, in particular, about their conception of the meaning or imminence of the eschatological Kingdom – but to wait for that 'baptism with the Holy Spirit' that would empower them to be his witnesses 'in Jerusalem, and all over Judea and Samaria, and away to the ends of the earth'. This corresponds with the command reported in Matthew 28:19 to 'go and make disciples of all nations', and the statement in Luke 24:47 that it was the divine plan that 'repentance and forgiveness of sins' should 'be preached to all nations, beginning at Jerusalem'. But the authenticity of any such instructions from the risen Lord is under widespread challenge today,[2] on a number of different grounds which are relevant to our subject.

The most obvious of these is the argument that, if Jesus had in fact given these instructions, it is difficult to understand the hesitations of the apostolic Church in regard to evangelising the Gentiles. I suppose that Peter's scruples about responding to the invitation of Cornelius could find a partial explanation in the 'table fellowship' that a visit to his house would almost inevitably involve, and that the controversy at the Council of Jerusalem turned primarily on whether Gentile converts should be required to be circumcised and to keep the Mosaic law.

However this may be, it seems clear that it was only after the Resurrection that Jesus gave these instructions; that he may not have spelt out their meaning in any detail; and that this would not be the only example of teaching which the disciples failed at the time to understand.

Another argument which is raised against the authenticity of these words (but which, at the same time, goes far to explain the controversies in the early Church about the Gentile mission) is the fact that Jesus not only saw his own mission of teaching and healing as directed, almost exclusively, to the Jews (cf. Matt. 15:24), but is reported as explicitly instructing the Twelve, when he sent them out on their mission: 'Do not take the road to Gentile lands, and do not enter any Samaritan town; but go rather to the lost sheep of the house of Israel' (Matt. 10:5f.).

It is, of course, recorded that he healed the daughter of a Syro-Phoenician woman (Mark 7:26) and the servant of a Roman centurion (Luke 7:1-10); that on one occasion he took his disciples through 'the borderlands of Samaria and Galilee' and healed a Samaritan leper (Luke 17:11-16); and that he won a number of converts in Samaria (John 4:4-42) – although at that time (in contrast to a somewhat earlier period) Samaritans were regarded by the Jews as very much on a par with Gentiles.[3]

But the paucity of material in the Gospel records about the Gentile mission – which was such a major subject of dispute and debate in the early Church – must surely testify, yet again, to the fact that the Evangelists were concerned to record the tradition of what Jesus actually taught, rather than to invent teaching that would have solved some of the Church's subsequent problems. How else can we explain the repeated emphasis in the Gospels on controversies about the Sabbath, and the lack of emphasis on circumcision, the Spirit and the Church?

It is abundantly clear that Jesus did not share the view, commonly accepted among his Jewish contemporaries, that the eschatological Kingdom would be reserved for Jews alone, or for Gentiles only in a subordinate and even servile capacity. On the contrary, Matthew reports his categorical statement – made, apparently, in the context of the Roman centurion's faith – that 'Many, I tell you, will come from east and west to feast with Abraham, Isaac and Jacob in the kingdom of Heaven. But those who were born to the kingdom will be driven out' (Matt. 8:11; cf. Luke 13:28f.). And after telling the

Parable of the Wicked Tenants, as we have seen, Matthew records that Jesus explicitly added: 'Therefore, I tell you, the Kingdom of God will be taken away from you, and given to a nation that yields the proper fruit' – words which the chief priests and Pharisees were not slow to understand (Matt. 21:43ff.).

This same point is implicit in several other parables, such as that of the Wedding Banquet (Matt. 22:1-10) and the Dinner Party (Luke 14:15-24).[4] On a number of occasions, too, Jesus is reported as referring to the 'world' rather than 'the house of Israel' – as in the interpretation of the parable of the Sower (Matt. 13:38) and some of the great Johannine sayings such as 'God loved the world so much that he gave his only Son, that everyone who has faith in him may not die but have eternal life. It was not to judge the world that God sent his Son into the world, but that through him the world might be saved' (John 3:16f.).

But when was the salvation of the Gentiles to take place? Joachim Jeremias argues that Jesus' words in Matthew 8:11f. and Luke 13:28f. – which he insists are early, and essentially Semitic – point to the day of final judgment, when the patriarchs and prophets will have risen and been seated in places of honour at the messianic banquet, and when God pronounces his sentence of judgment on those 'sons of the Kingdom' who are to be excluded. It is then, and only then, Jeremias asserts, that Jesus envisaged that 'Men [Gentiles] will come from east and west, and from north and south, and sit at table in the kingdom of God' (Luke 13:28); and he believes that Jesus derived this vision from passages such as Isaiah 2:2f., where he must have read the prophecy:

And it shall come to pass in the latter days, that the mountain of the Lord's house shall be established in the top of the mountains, and shall be exalted above the hills; and all nations shall flow unto it; and many peoples shall go and say, Come ye, and let us go up to the mountain of the Lord, to the house of the God of Jacob; and he will teach us of his ways ... (*Promise*, p. 56).

On the basis of passages such as this, many of which he quotes, Jeremias insists that, in the Old Testament, 'the eschatological pilgrimage of the Gentiles' is always to 'Zion, the Holy Mountain of God', and that *'the Gentiles will not be evangelised where they dwell, but will be summoned to the holy Mount by the divine epiphany'* (*Promise*, p. 60; my italics). As a consequence he attempts to force all the recorded logia about the proclamation of the Gospel to the Gentiles into this same mould. Thus he interprets the saying in Mark 14:9 about the woman who anointed Jesus at Bethany as meaning that 'when the triumphal news is proclaimed (by God's angel) to all the world, then will her act be remembered (before God), so that he may be gracious to her (at the last judgment)'; and he suggests that

> a similar interpretation should be given to the closely-related isolated saying in Mark 13:10 which read in its original Matthean form: 'And this gospel of the kingdom shall be preached in the whole world for a testimony unto all the nations; and then shall the end come' (Matt. 24:14). Here, too, the original reference is not to human proclamation, but to an apocalyptic event, namely, angelic proclamation of God's final act (*Promise*, pp. 22f.).

This represents a combination of speculation and special pleading that I find singularly unconvincing – implying that the apostles completely misunderstood their Master's words when, under the teaching of the Holy Spirit, they saw it as their duty not to wait for an eschatological 'ingathering of the Gentiles' to hear the angelic proclamation of 'the triumphal news' at the Parousia, but to take the Gospel to the Gentiles with human lips and eager urgency. Were the first Christians, then, much more enlightened than Jesus himself when they saw a symbolic meaning, applicable to the days of the New Covenant, in a number of Old Testament passages and concepts?[5]

It is significant in this context that Jeremias rightly insists that the 'ingathering of the Gentiles' could come only after the Passion and Resurrection. Quoting from John's Gospel, he emphasises that it was when Gentiles sought him out, late in his ministry, that Jesus said: 'The hour has come for the Son of Man to be glorified', and immediately added: 'In truth, in very truth I tell you, a grain of wheat remains a solitary grain unless it falls into the ground and dies; but if it dies, it bears a rich harvest' (John 12:23f.). So, Jeremias writes,

> Not until he is lifted up from the earth will he draw all men unto him (12:32; cf. 11:51f.) . . . It is not by accident that the saying in John 10:16 about the 'other sheep' comes after the announcement of his laying down his life (v. 15). Hence the Fourth Gospel repeatedly emphasises the fact that the hour of the Gentiles . . . can only come after the Cross (*Promise*, pp. 37f.).

Jeremias also observes that this same truth – that the time of the Gentiles must come after the Passion – is unmistakably implicit in the synoptic Gospels. 'The words of Jesus at the Last Supper make it clear that this was in the mind of Jesus. The blood of the true passover Lamb must first be shed "for many" (Mark 14:24), the ransom must be paid "for many" (Mark 10:45), namely, for the countless hosts from all nations (Isa. 53:11f.), before the universal Kingdom of God could arrive' (*Promise*, pp. 72f.). This very point makes it all the more difficult to see why there is such a weight of scholarly reluctance to believe that, even *after the Passion*, the risen Lord could have given his disciples a world-wide mission of evangelism which was essentially different from the strictly circumscribed missions on which he had sent them during his earthly ministry – slow though the Church was to grasp the full import of words he may not have seen fit to elucidate at the time, knowing that the promised Holy Spirit would shed an increasing light on their meaning and implications.

The Imminence of the Parousia

The major reason, I think, for this scholarly reluctance is the widely held belief that Jesus himself not only expected, but explicitly predicted, that his Parousia would take place during the life-time of some of his own generation. For this belief a considerable number of logia are commonly cited: e.g. Mark 9:1 (cf. Matt. 16:28; Luke 9:27); Mark 13:28ff. (cf. Matt. 24:32-5; Luke 21:29-32); Mark 14:62 (cf. Matt. 26:64; Luke 22:69); and Matthew 10:23. It is true that the authenticity of some of these sayings has been challenged; but it seems strange that so many scholars who accept their essential authenticity place such reliance on one particular interpretation of them (the validity of which inevitably hinges on the precise form, context and reference in which they have been reported) that they reject out of hand other recorded logia which suggest a different, and by no means impossible, exegesis. Volumes have been written on this subject, which I can do no more than touch on here.

The first group of sayings (Mark 9:1 and parallels) all occur just after Peter's confession of faith at Caesarea Philippi and Jesus' warning to his disciples of coming suffering – both for him as Son of Man and for them as his followers. But they must not falter in their witness or disown him, for one day he would come 'in the glory of the Father with his angels' to give every man his due reward (Matt. 16:27; cf. Mark 8:38; Luke 9:26). It was in this context that he spoke words of encouragement, assuring them that 'some of those standing here will not taste of death before they have seen the Kingdom of God' (Luke 9:27); 'before they have seen the Kingdom of God already come in power' (Mark 9:1); or 'before they have seen the Son of Man coming in his Kingdom' (Matt. 11:28).

Thus the element common to all three Gospels is a reference to the coming of the Kingdom. This would, indeed, only be consummated at the Parousia; but it would be rash to conclude that the promise in Mark 9:1 and parallels *must* mean that this final consummation would take place during the life-time of some of those addressed. In all the synoptic Gospels this logion is immediately followed by the Transfiguration, with which Mark seems specifically to link it – as, presumably, a unique foretaste of the way in which the glory already inherent

(although veiled) in Jesus would ultimately be fully revealed
(2 Pet. 1:16-18; cf. 1 Pet. 5:1).

To dismiss this interpretation as absurd, on the ground that
it would be meaningless for Jesus to say that 'some of those
standing here' would not die before an event which in fact, we
are told, happened only six days later, presupposes that he
himself knew both *how* his prediction would be fulfilled, and
when this would be. This, however, is by no means certain.
What is clear is that he is reported as explicitly stating that he
did *not* know the date of the Parousia (Mark 13:32; Matt.
24:36). The Kingdom (already present, as we have seen, in the
person of Jesus) was to 'come in power' at the 'exodus' (death,
resurrection and ascension) that 'he was to accomplish in
Jerusalem', about which Luke records that he conversed with
Moses and Elijah on the mount of Transfiguration. It was to
come in power, too, at Pentecost; in judgment and warning at
the Fall of Jerusalem; and in salvation in the ever widening
witness of the Church. In a very real sense the coming of the
Kingdom is inextricably linked with a 'coming' of Jesus
himself: in his mission, death, resurrection and exaltation; in
his 'return' to his bereft disciples in the person of the 'other
Counsellor'; in his predicted judgment on the city and nation
that had rejected him; and also, pre-eminently, in his final
intervention, both in salvation and in judgment, at the end of
the age. This would happen when God's hour struck, but at a
date about which the incarnate Son himself declared his
ignorance (cf. Cranfield, *Mark*, p. 288).

It is appropriate to turn next to the third group of logia
mentioned above. This group concerns the reply Jesus, on oath
at his trial, is reported as giving to the question put to him by
the High Priest: 'Are you the Messiah, the Son of the Blessed
One?' In Mark's record, as we have seen (p. 154), Jesus replied:
'I am; and you will see the Son of Man seated at the right hand
of God and coming with the clouds of heaven' (Mark 14:62).
Matthew's record is closely similar, while Luke reports that
Jesus, after making the same confession as to who he was (but
in the somewhat more reserved words which Matthew also
records) affirmed that 'from henceforth [or, *possibly*, 'cer-

tainly'] you will see the Son of Man seated at the right hand of God and coming on the clouds of heaven' (Matt. 26:64; cf. Luke 22:69). Here the contrast is between the lowly status of Jesus 'now' at his trial and the glory that would be revealed at his Parousia *whenever that should occur*. The High Priest and members of the Sanhedrin would see this indeed, but not necessarily during their earthly lives.[6]

It is the second group of sayings (Mark 13:28f. and parallels) which gives rise to the greatest controversy. In these, as in the first group, we find an emphatic statement, in all the synoptic Gospels, that 'this generation will certainly not pass away until all these things have happened'; but it is by no means easy to decide to what, precisely, these words refer.

The immediate context, in the 'Eschatological Discourse' recorded in Matthew 24, Mark 13 and Luke 21, is that Jesus was giving his answer to two distinct questions put to him by his disciples: first, when the destruction of the Temple (which he had just predicted) would happen; second, 'What will be the signal for your coming and the end of the age?' (Matt. 24:3 – but probably implicit, too, in the other Gospels). In his reply Jesus seems to have predicted the comparative imminence of the Fall of Jerusalem (Luke 21:20-4. Cf. Mark 13:14ff.; Matt. 24:15ff.).[7] But the statement in Luke 21:24 that, after this, 'Jerusalem will be trampled down by foreigners until their day has run its course' seems to point to a period of indefinite duration between this event and the end of the age – which, again, was to be accompanied or preceded by certain 'portents' described in apocalyptic terms (cf. Matt. 24:29ff; Mark 13:24ff.; Luke 21:25ff.) – whether these are to be understood literally or figuratively.

To what, then, does the emphatic allusion to 'this generation', in all these Gospels, actually refer? It has been said that the word *genea* can mean: '(a) the descendants of a common ancestor; (b) a set of people born at the same time; (c) the period of time occupied by such a set of people' (Marshall, *Luke*, p. 780) – so the meaning of the term is flexible, and it has, in fact, been understood in a variety of different senses in this context.

Some commentators have concluded that the reference here is to the Jewish race (as a 'word of hope' that God will not reject them utterly 'but give them a share in final salvation').[8] Others have taken it to refer to 'this type, namely the perverse and faithless'.[9] If, however, the phrase is to be taken in a chronological sense, there are still a variety of possibilities. It might refer to the 'generation of the end signs'[10] – i.e. that those who saw the signs would live to see the end itself; and in support of this view Ellis observes that the usage of the Qumran community

> indicates that in the New Testament 'this (last) generation', like 'last hour' (1 Jn. 2:18) or 'today', means only the last phase in the history of redemption. None of the terms are to be understood in a literal way. The public revelation of the kingdom *is* just round the corner, but its calendar time is left indeterminate (*Luke*, pp. 246f.).

And if – as most commentators believe – the reference was to Jesus' own contemporaries exclusively, then there is a very strong possibility, or probability, that what he said they would live to see, and should pray for strength to 'pass safely through' (Luke 21:36), were the 'imminent troubles' and portents of the Parousia, not the Parousia itself (cf. Caird, *Luke*, pp. 233f.). So the common assumption that he mistakenly predicted (or was understood to predict) that the Parousia would take place before all his contemporaries had died, is open to very serious challenge. To this we must return.

Matthew 10:23, which remains to be considered, is a difficult verse. The context is that of the Matthean version of Jesus' charge to the Twelve when he sent them out, two by two, on a temporary mission of teaching and healing as part of their training. They were to travel light and depend on the hospitality they would receive – as is recorded, with minor differences in wording, in Matthew 10, Mark 6 and Luke 9 (cf. also Luke 10, for the very similar charge to the Seventy, or Seventy-two).

In Matthew 10 verses 5-8 and 40-2 are peculiar to Matthew;

verses 17-25 have parallels in the eschatological discourses in Mark 13 and Luke 21; verses 26-30 have no parallels in Mark, but are found in four different places in Luke (12:2-9, 51-3; 14:26f. and 17:33).[11] No doubt Jesus, like any good teacher, must often have repeated the same or similar teaching on different occasions; but it seems obvious that a considerable part of the material in Matthew 10:5-42 was not relevant to this particular mission, and it is probable that Matthew included in this chapter certain warnings and instructions whose primary reference was to witness and evangelism in a much wider context.

This makes it far from clear to what, precisely, verse 23 refers. It can, in any case, scarcely refer exclusively to the immediate mission of the Twelve, which seems to have been of quite short duration, and to which verses 17-22 can hardly apply. The return of the Twelve to Jesus, reported in Mark 6:30, does not necessarily mean that they did not subsequently resume their itinerant ministry – so the words: 'I tell you this; you will not have gone through all the towns of Israel before the Son of Man comes' may well mean that they would not have completed their mission of strictly Israel-orientated evangelism before the Son of Man came back to them, risen from the dead, to give them a much wider commission (cf. Tasker, *Matthew*, p. 108), or before he had come in judgment on Israel in the destruction of Jerusalem in A.D.70. Thus Kümmel suggests that this passage in Matthew refers to the apostles' 'completion of their missionary task ... with regard to their nation' (*Promise*, p. 62). But if the commission in verses 5-42 is composite, and includes in its scope the Church's mission to the Jews of the Dispersion and also to the Gentile world (as seems to me very probable),[12] then Kümmel goes much too far in asserting that verse 23 'confirms the conclusion that Jesus reckoned on the coming of the Kingdom of God and the Son of Man in glory [in the Parousia] within the lifetime of the generation of his hearers' (*Promise*, p. 64).

Any such conclusion would necessarily involve one of two alternatives: either that Jesus made a positive prediction which was falsified by history, or that the Evangelists misunderstood his teaching – or, indeed, attributed to him teaching he had never given. But we have already noted that Mark 13:32 (cf. Matt. 24:36) provides very strong evidence that Jesus specifically denied that he knew when 'that day' would come; such knowledge belonged to the Father alone. So it seems intrinsically unlikely that he would have stated categorically that it would be within the span of a single generation. It is, of course, possible that this seemed to him probable, for the incarnate Lord was not omniscient; but he repeatedly insists in John's Gospel, in the most unequivocal terms, that what he actually *taught* was exclusively what had been revealed to him by his Father and communicated by his command (cf. p. 156 above).

The Eschatological Discourse

The alleged difficulty in interpreting the Eschatological Discourse in the synoptic Gospels in a way which reconciles Mark 13:32 (cf. Matt. 24:36) with Mark 13:30 (and parallels) seems to me greatly exaggerated. In this context I find an analysis of Mark 13 by David Wenham[13] very persuasive – although it must be conceded that, on *any* analysis, the meaning of a number of points in this discourse remains elusive and uncertain.

Wenham suggests that Jesus' answer to the disciples' question falls into two main parts (verses 5-27 and 28-37, respectively). The first of these passages provides a summarised outline of the whole sequence of events leading up to, and including, the end of the age, and is itself subdivided into two distinct sections: (a) verses 5-23 and (b) verses 24-7. Verses 5-23 – described by Cranfield (*Mark*, p. 394) as 'The Characteristics of the Last Times' or 'The Signs of the End' (which verse 7 declares is 'not yet') – refer to impostors, battles, earthquakes, famines, persecutions, sufferings and family divisions, against the background of the Gospel being preached to all nations (v. 10; cf. Matt. 24:14); and they give particular emphasis to 'The Abomination of Desolation' (vv.

14-23), in which I again follow Cranfield in seeing a double reference: first, to the fate that would soon befall Jerusalem and its Temple, and second, to the final 'Antichrist' who would immediately precede the End (cf. 2 Thess. 2:3-10). Verses 24-7 (another distinct unit), on the other hand, refer to the Parousia itself together with the portents, whether literal or figurative, that accompany or precede it.

Then the second main part of this discourse represents Jesus' direct answer to the disciples' recorded question about the timing of these events; and this can be subdivided into three sections. In verses 28f. Jesus shows how the two distinct sections of the first part of his reply (centring on the 'Abomination of Desolation' and the Parousia, respectively) are inter-related, the first pointing forward to the second. In verses 30f. he emphatically declares that some of his own generation will live 'to see all this happening' (that is, what is described in vv. 5-23). Finally, in verses 32-7 he turns to the Parousia itself, and first states unequivocally that the time when 'that day' will come is known to the Father alone (and even the Son does not share this knowledge), and then draws certain spiritual lessons – the imperative need for watchfulness, diligence and expectancy.

No doubt the Evangelists themselves would have been astonished if anyone could have told them what a long gap would elapse between the 'Abomination of Desolation' and its preceding and subsequent sufferings – not all of them, by any means, confined to Palestine – and the 'End' to which it served as a principal pointer. But this knowledge, even if anyone could have given them it, would have impoverished rather than enriched the lives and witness of their readers down the centuries. The point at issue is, however, not what the Evangelists (or even Jesus himself) expected, but what Jesus explicitly predicted.

Since nothing else in the reported teaching of Jesus has, perhaps, given rise to more scholarly debate and controversy than this eschatological discourse in the synoptic Gospels, it seems appropriate to add a few further comments. The accounts in Matthew 24 and Luke 21 follow the broad outline of Mark 13 and include a number of verses which seem clearly to be derived from that chapter (or the traditions on which it rests), while the differences from it can be explained partly in terms of redaction and elucidation, and partly in terms of dependence on an independent source (or even a very early source available to them all). Wenham's analysis of Mark 13 appears to be almost equally applicable to the other Synoptists' summary of this discourse, while it is abundantly clear, as he observes, that no strictly chronological sequence of the phenomena mentioned in these chapters can be postulated. An illustration of this can be seen in Matthew 24, with cross references to Luke 21. Thus Matthew 24:14 states that 'this gospel of the Kingdom will be proclaimed throughout the earth as a testimony to all nations, and then the end will come'; verses 15ff. refer to the 'abomination of desolation' (cf. Luke 21:20, which refers explicitly to Jerusalem); while verses 27ff. make it clear that, whatever questioning and uncertainty may precede it, the Parousia itself will be quite unmistakable.

Again, it seems clear that, on the most natural translation of Matthew 24:34 ('I tell you the truth, this generation will certainly not pass away until all these things have happened'), the 'all things' referred to must be identical with 'all these things' in the immediately preceding verse; for it would not make sense to suggest that verse 33 means that 'when you see all these things [*including* the Parousia itself], you may know that it [or he] is near, right at the door'. So what some of Jesus' generation would live to see would be the *signs* of the imminence of the Advent (and, in particular, the destruction of Jerusalem), rather than the Advent itself, the time of which was known to the Father alone (vv. 36ff.).

Somewhat similarly, Luke 21:25f. speaks of 'portents' which will cause men to 'faint with terror at the thought of all that is coming upon the world; for the celestial powers will be shaken. And then they shall see the Son of Man coming on a cloud with great power and glory', whereas verse 28 reads: 'When all this *begins* to happen, stand upright and hold your heads high, because your liberation is near'. So when verse 32 adds: 'I tell you this, this generation will not pass away until all this has happened', the meaning of 'all this' would seem to be the beginning of the End rather than the final event itself.

Cranfield's 'tentative conclusion' is that Mark 13:5-37 'does give us substantially our Lord's teaching', although that 'does not mean that we can be certain that throughout the discourse we have his exact words. Nor is it implied that it was uttered as a single discourse'. He insists that it 'differs radically from typical Jewish apocalyptic. While the language of apocalyptic is indeed used, the purpose for which it is used and even the form of the discourse are different . . . It is in fact exhortation, not ordinary apocalyptic. Its purpose is not to impart esoteric information, but to sustain faith and obedience'. He emphasises that we must recognise two tensions: the first, between the explicit warning against trying to know the date of the End (v.32) and 'all that is said about the signs of the end' (vv. 5-23); the second, between the statements that 'the end is not yet' (v. 7) and 'the Gospel must first be preached to all the nations' (v. 10), on the one hand, and the equally explicit affirmation that 'when you see all this happening, you may know that he is near, even at the doors' (v. 29), on the other. It is vital in both cases, he maintains, to hold 'the two elements of the paradox' together, 'so that each may control, and help to interpret, the other' (*Mark*, pp. 388f.).

The End of the Age

Thus Cranfield's analysis of Mark 13 does not differ greatly in substance from Wenham's, although there are minor differences. He comments on vv. 26f. (which 'speak of the Parousia itself and the gathering of the elect') that: 'The End-event will be the coming in glory of him "who at that time was living on earth in the garb of a despised servant" (Calvin) (cf. 8:38, 14:62)'; on v. 29 that: 'Strictly the reference of *tauta* [these things] should include the coming of the Son of Man mentioned in v. 26; but, as the sense would then be, "When you see the Son of Man coming, know that he is at hand", which would be pointless, it is better to refer it to the signs of the End described in vv. 5-23'; and on verse 32 that: 'An assertion of Jesus' ignorance is unlikely to have been created by the Church. Even had the early community been as embarrassed by the so-called "delay of the Parousia" as some allege, less uncongenial expedients for explaining away its embarrassment would surely have been available' (*Mark*, pp. 406f., 410). In any case, he aptly observes that

> If we realise that the Incarnation-Crucifixion-Resurrection-Ascension, on the one hand, and the Parousia, on the other, belong essentially together and are in a real sense one Event, one divine Act, being held apart only by the mercy of God who desires to give man opportunity for faith and repentance, then we can see that in a very real sense the latter is always imminent now that the former has happened. It was, and still is, true to say that the Parousia is at hand – and indeed this, far from being an embarrassing mistake on the part either of Jesus or of the early Church, is an essential part of the Church's faith. Ever since the Incarnation men have been living in the last days' (*Mark*, p. 408).

The Parousia is, of course, only one of the words used in the New Testament for 'Christ's Messianic Advent in glory to judge the world at the end of the age' (B.A.G.) In the contemporary Greek it had become the official term for a 'royal' visit, presence or arrival; it is the word used in Matthew 24:3 to translate the disciples' question about the 'signal' for his 'coming'; and it is found over twenty times in the New Testament. But the term *apokalypsis* (unveiling) and *epiphaneia* (appearing) are also used in this same context. We have already noted a number of references to this coming in glory in which Jesus is reported to have said that he will then 'send out his angels, and they will gather his chosen from the four winds, from the farthest bounds of heaven on every side' (Matt. 24:31; cf. Mark 13:26f.). The technical term for this is the 'Rapture'.[14] It is then, too, that the Son of Man will preside over the 'Day of judgment' (Matt. 16:27; 25:31; etc.). In John's Gospel Jesus explicitly states that the Father himself 'judges no one, but has entrusted all judgment to the Son' specifically 'because he is the Son of Man' (John 5:22 and 27). Then 'all who are in the grave will hear his voice and come forth; those who have done right will rise to life; those who have done wrong will rise to their doom' (John 5:28f.).

The criteria for this judgment will be utterly just, for all 'secrets' will then be known (Luke 8:17); and the verdict of acquittal or condemnation will depend, in the ultimate analysis, on the righteousness that a holy God must require, on the one hand, and on our response to the message of his redeeming love in Christ, as communicated to us by him or by his 'brothers' (cf. Matt. 25:31-46; and pp. 52f. above), on the other.

Thus Jesus is reported in John 5:24 as stating: 'In very truth, anyone who gives heed to what I say and puts his trust in him who sent me has eternal life and will not be condemned; he has already crossed over from death to life'; and in Matthew 10:32f.: 'Whoever acknowledges me before men, I will also acknowledge him before my Father in heaven. But whoever disowns me before men, I will disown him before my Father in heaven'. This is spelt out in the words of John 3:16-19:

> For God so loved the world that he gave his one and only Son, that whoever believes in him shall not perish but have eternal life. For God did not send his Son into the world to condemn the world, but that through him the world might be saved. Whoever puts his faith in him does not come under condemnation; but whoever does not believe in him stands condemned already, because he has not believed in God's one and only Son. Here lies the test: the light has come into the world, but men preferred darkness to light because their deeds were evil.[15]

The result of the Judgment is either 'Heaven' or 'Hell'. Hell is usually depicted in the Bible in symbolic terms (cf. pp. 74, 89f. above). Its essential meaning is deprivation or loss: to be excluded from the presence of God, and thus from 'eternal life' (cf. Matt. 7:23; John 5:25-9). It is described as 'eternal' (primarily, at least) because it represents a judgment which is final and irreversible.[16] The imagery in which it is described in Mark 9:47f., and repeatedly in Matthew[17], is derived from Isaiah 66:24 and 34:9f. This is certainly not to be interpreted in a literal sense, and should probably be understood in terms of eternal destruction (Matt. 10:28; cf. 2 Thess. 1:9) rather than endless torment – although we must never minimise the horror of this sentence of condemnation, which may well be proportionate rather than uniform (cf. Luke 12:47f.). But Dr. R. J. Bauckham aptly insists that

> It is important to notice that there is no symmetry about the two destinies of men: the Kingdom of God has been prepared for the redeemed (Matt. 25:34), but hell has been prepared for the devil and his angels (Matt. 25:41) and becomes the fate of men only because they have refused their true destiny which God offers them in Christ. The N. T. doctrine of hell, like all N. T. eschatology, is never mere information; it is a warning given in the context of the Gospel's call to repentance and faith in Christ.[18]

Heaven, too, is largely described in parabolic terms – for how can something quite beyond all human experience be spelt out in human words? Thus we have the parables of the Messianic 'Banquet' (Luke 14:15-24), the Pounds (Luke 19:11-19), and the Talents (Matt. 25:14-23), together with the vivid imagery of Revelation 21 and 22. In much more simple terms, John reports that Jesus told his disciples:

> There are many dwelling-places in my Father's house; if it were not so I should have told you; for I am going on purpose to prepare a place for you. And if I go and prepare a place for you, I shall come again and receive you to myself, so that where I am you may be also (John 14:2f.).

It seems to me probable that John Marsh is right when he suggests that Jesus was about to 'prepare a place' for them (and us) primarily by the very act and manner of his 'going': that is, by his atoning death on the Cross (*John*, p. 501). But the words 'I shall come again and receive you to myself, so that where I am you may be also' seem to point directly to the Parousia. In the New Testament, as we have seen, this is always depicted as imminent, for the eschatological Kingdom has already been inaugurated in the person and ministry of Jesus and now only awaits its consummation. So the emphasis is constantly on watchfulness, industry and endurance.[19] That is one reason why Jesus told his disciples – and, through them, the Church down the ages – continually to celebrate the 'Lord's Supper', in remembrance of his atoning death and the New Covenant sealed by his blood, 'until he comes' (1 Cor. 11:26; cf. Matt. 26:29; Mark 14:25). To this our glad response should be 'Amen. Come, Lord Jesus' (Rev. 22:20).

Epilogue

I can well imagine some people, whether they have persevered with this book to the end or merely flipped through its pages, being somewhat surprised that no separate section has been devoted to what is often cited as the very essence of the teaching of Jesus: the universal fatherhood of God and brotherhood of man. So I want to bring together in this Epilogue some of the implications of many scattered references to this subject.

Numerous quotations from the Gospels have, I hope, made it abundantly clear that Jesus revealed God as his own Father, and also his disciples' Father, in a way that was startlingly new. The thought of God as in one sense 'father' of Israel's king, and of Israel as a nation, was certainly familiar to the Old Testament writers (as 2 Sam. 7:14, Isa. 63:16 and Jer. 31:9 testify), and this concept was further developed during the inter-testamental period, where we read in the Book of Jubilees, for example, that God said of spiritual or 'righteous' Israelites 'I will be their Father and they shall be my sons' (Jubilees 1:24).[1] But although it was a characteristic of Hasidic piety to think of God as 'Father in heaven' (Vermēs, *Jesus the Jew*, p. 210), it can be said with confidence that no one before Jesus made it his practice to address the Almighty simply as 'Father', habitually (it seems) using the affectionately familiar Aramaic term 'Abba' which was used by children only within the family circle. It was, in fact, the distinctive personal relationship that Jesus, as 'the Son', claimed with 'the Father' that was the reason for much of the opposition, and accusations of blasphemy, that he encountered.

But while Jesus must have realised, at a very early age (see pp. 156ff. above), that his intimate relationship with his Father was unique, he continually spoke to his disciples about 'your Father', or 'your heavenly Father', and taught them to pray to him as such. This is clearly reflected in the fact that Paul, in two letters written to largely Gentile churches, declared that God had sent 'the Spirit of his Son' into their hearts, crying 'Abba, Father!' (Gal. 4:6; cf. Rom. 8:15). The only convincing reason for the introduction of this Aramaic word into the Greek of these letters is that it must have been a lingering echo of Jesus' own well remembered practice. And Jesus repeatedly taught his disciples the corollary truth that, if they were all sons of the same Father, then their relationship to each other must be that of brothers (Matt. 23:8).

But did Jesus in fact teach 'the universal fatherhood of God and brotherhood of man'?[2] It is certainly clear that Paul taught that the nature of God is that of a father, for fatherhood is not a human relationship which we attribute to God, but the essential relationship of God to his people which human fathers only dimly reflect (cf. Eph. 3:14f.). Paul is also reported to have told the Athenians that God had 'created every race of men of one stock'. So all men are not only inter-related; they are God's 'offspring' (Acts 17:25, 28). But in what sense is this derived from the teaching of Jesus?

The answer is, I think, twofold, as both Paul and the Church perceived. Jesus himself taught that the very nature of God was that of a father-creator who 'causes his sun to rise on the evil and the good, and sends rain on the righteous and the unrighteous' (Matt. 5:45). Without his knowledge not even a sparrow can 'fall to the ground' (Matt. 10:29). He told the Samaritan woman that 'the time approaches, indeed it is already here, when those who are true worshippers will worship the Father in spirit and in truth. Such are the worshippers whom the Father wants' (John 4:23); and he assured his disciples that 'it is not your heavenly Father's will that one of these little ones should be lost' (Matt. 18:24).

Yet he also taught that a true family relationship with God was not inherent in all men by the fact that they had been created by him in his own 'image and likeness', but that the status of being a 'son of God' was acquired, or rather bestowed, only by means of their relationship with the eternal Son (Matt. 11:27; John 14:6). Thus Paul reminded the Galatians that 'You are all sons of God through faith in Christ Jesus' (Gal. 3:26) and John writes of Jesus:

> He, through whom the world was made, was in the world, and the world treated him as a stranger. He came to what was his own, and they who were his own gave him no welcome. But all those who did welcome him he empowered to become children of God, all those who believe in his name; their birth came, not from human stock, not from nature's will or man's, but from God (John 1:10ff. Knox).

On one occasion he said to his critics: 'If God were your Father you would love me, for I came from God', and then added: 'You belong to your father, the devil' (John 8:42ff.). This is why – in terms of the central emphasis of this book – Jesus insisted, in his talk with Nicodemus, that no one can enter or even 'see' the Kingdom of God unless and until he has been 'born anew' (or 'from above') by repentance and spiritual regeneration (John 3:3–5). In other words, it is only when a man accepts the kingly rule of God that he comes to know that the King is, in fact, his Father.[3]

Two further points follow. First, while it is gloriously true that God loves the whole world with a love we cannot begin to comprehend, he has a special relationship with those who have responded to his love (John 14:21, 23; 17:23). Similarly, we read that 'the living God is the Saviour of all men, and especially of those who believe' (1 Tim. 4:10). And the corollary of this is that while Christians should love all men, made (as they are) 'in God's likeness', and should extend their care to all who are 'poor' or in any sort of need, it is both natural and right that they should have a particular love for the 'brotherhood' of fellow believers, as members of their own spiritual family. With them they have a special – but by no means exclusive – duty to 'share' both the spiritual and material gifts which they have themselves received from 'the Father of the heavenly lights, who does not change like shifting shadows' (James 1:17).

Secondly, this helps to clarify the relationship between the Kingdom of God and his Church. The Kingdom and the

Church are not by any means identical, yet they are very closely related. The Kingdom is not confined to the Church, for it comprises the whole sphere of God's kingly activity (cf. Mark 4:26–9). But it is those who have already accepted God's kingly rule who both enjoy and provide a foretaste of the Kingdom that will one day be universal, just as it is only those who have received the 'Spirit of his Son' who can (and do) cry 'Abba! Father!'

In the final analysis, the true citizens of the Kingdom are all sons of the King – a 'royal priesthood' (Rev. 1:6; 5:10) – to whom 'the Father has chosen to give the Kingdom' (Luke 12:32).

Notes

Full bibliographical details may be found in the List of Authors cited

Chapter 1

1 Cf. Arthur Jeffery, 'The Textual History of the Qur'ān', in his *Qur'ān*, pp. 89–103, especially pp. 93ff. We know, for example, that the Codex of Ibn Mas'ūd, which was highly regarded in Kūfa, omitted Sūras 1, 113 and 114, while both that of Abū Mūsā and that of Ubai (widely accepted in Baṣra and in the greater part of Syria, respectively) included two short sūras which were not incorporated in the official Recension.

2 The Muslim era is dated from the year of Muhammad's 'emigration' from Mecca to Madina, some ten years before his death. The Hijra took place in A.D. 622; but Muslims observe lunar rather than solar years, which means that the transposition of subsequent dates is far from simple.

3 Some order in the resulting chaos had been produced, in the Caliphate of 'Abd al-Mālik, by al-Ḥajjāj b. Yūsuf (who seems to have been responsible for what was almost a new Recension of the Qur'ān); and in A.H. 322 it was decreed that only seven systems of pointing and vowelling the unpointed and unvowelled text were thenceforth to be permitted. Even so, the claims of certain other systems were championed for a time, and variants within the 'canonical seven' duly appeared (cf. Jeffery, *Qur'ān*, pp. 97f.).

4 Although it is true that the first substantial appearance of *aḥādīth* in written form (but without a formal *isnād*, etc.) was in the *Muwatta* of Malik b. Anas, who died A.H. 179 –

i.e. some 160 years after the Prophet's death.

5 Cf. Joseph Schacht, *Origins*, p. 4.

6 Cf. Noel J. Coulson, *History*, pp. 64ff.

7 Except, of course, the apocryphal gospels.

8 A strong case for the circulation of some of the teaching of Jesus in written form (some of it possibly in Greek) has been made by E. Earle Ellis in *Prophecy and Hermeneutic* pp. 243–7.

9 Davies, *Setting*, p. 417. Cf. Marshall, *Historical Jesus*, p. 194. Barrett, *Gospel Tradition* (pp. 10f.) seems to me to over-react to Gerhardsson's views.

10 'Form-criticism' attempts to analyse and classify the discrete units in which the sayings of Jesus and stories about him were communicated orally before they came to be incorporated in our Gospels. 'Redaction-criticism' focuses on the way in which the Evangelists 'edited' and arranged the traditional material they received and used. Cf. a series of articles in *New Testament Interpretation* (ed. I. H. Marshall).

11 Some of which were written at a date as far removed from the life of Jesus as the *aḥādīth* literature from the life of Muhammad.

Chapter 2

1 Or, in the typically Jewish paraphrase usually preferred by Matthew (which may well represent the Aramaic original), the 'Kingdom of the heavens'.

2 In this respect, *inter alia*, it is clear that the book of Daniel is much closer to the Old Testament prophets than to the later apocalyptists.

3 Cf. *Commentary on Habakkuk*, 7:1–5 and *Manual of Discipline*, 9:9. (Cf. Ladd, *Presence*, pp. 81, 105, 223).

4 E.g. R. V. G. Tasker, *Matthew*, pp. 118f.

5 Mark 10:45; Matt. 20:28. Cranfield (*Mark*, pp. 342f.) believes that the Hebrew word for 'guilt-offering' (Lev.

5:14; 6:7; 7:1–7; Num. 5:5–8) probably underlies the Greek *lutron* here (although *lutron* is not used in these passages in the Septuagint), since it would seem that Jesus had Isa. 53:10 in mind ('when thou shalt make his soul an *offering for* sin'). He also emphasises that *anti pollōn* here means not 'on behalf of', but 'in place of', and seems to echo Isa. 53:11f. C. K. Barrett, Morna Hooker and others have argued strongly against this interpretation; but I remain unconvinced.

6 The less well attested reading, 'You say that I am', accords with Matthew 26:64 and Luke 22:70 (and also Mark 15:2). In any case the meaning is virtually the same.

7 In Matt. 13 and 18; Mark 4; and Luke 8:1–18 and 13:18–21.

8 Which, Jeremias insists, is the basic meaning of Mark 4:11(b) (*Parables*, p. 14).

9 In Mark 4:12 '*hina*' is translated in N.E.B. 'so that [as Scripture says] ...' Cf. W. L. Lane, *Mark*, pp. 158f. Jeremias (*Parables*, pp. 14f.) prefers 'in order that' and regards '*hina*' here as virtually an abbreviation of '*hina plērōthēi*' ('that it may be fulfilled ...').

10 Cf. John Marsh, *John*, p. 471.

11 On this point cf. T. W. Manson, *Teaching*, pp. 76, 79f. Also, on the whole parable and its interpretation, C. F. D. Moule 'Mark 4:1–20. Yet once more', in *Neotestamentica et Semitica*, pp. 95–113.

12 This is the sort of point in which a parable must certainly be distinguished from an allegory.

13 Cf. Jer. 7:25f.; 25:4; Josh. 14:7; Amos 3:7 and Zeph. 1:4 – on which Cranfield makes the pertinent comment: 'Is it conceivable that Jesus could take up the O.T. figure of God's vineyard and then speak of the owner sending his slaves one after another without thinking of the prophets?' (*Mark*, p. 367).

14 It is noteworthy that J. D. M. Derrett, who regards these two parables as variants on the same basic theme, insists that in Matt. 22 'The allegedly separate little parable of the man who came without a wedding garment turns out to be an actual, or at least an inherent, or potential, part of the

main parable'. He also gives a whole series of 'Suggested Solutions for Difficulties' in the story. Cf. *Law*, pp. 126, 142f., 153ff.

Chapter 3

1 A very full bibliography and discussion of the different views which scholars have taken on this controversial subject can be found in G. E. Ladd, *Presence*.
2 T. W. Manson, 'Cleansing', p. 279.
3 So similar, in fact, that many scholars regard the two as 'doublets'. But E. E. Ellis (*Luke*, p. 154) justly describes the mission of the Seventy as 'a parallel to the earlier mission of the Twelve'.
4 Precisely the same question was asked, in Luke 10:25, by 'an expert in the law'; and there led on to the parable of the Good Samaritan.
5 There is, of course, much speculation as to the point in this chapter at which the Evangelist turns from words he attributes to Jesus to his own reflection on their meaning.
6 E.g. I. H. Marshall, *Luke*, p. 698.
7 Cf. Acts 5:31 and 11:18; Rom. 2:4; 2 Tim. 2:25.
8 Cf. 1 Pet. 1:4f. for the double preservation of the inheritance for its heirs and of the heirs for their inheritance.
9 Cf. Matt. 26:13; John 3:16; Matt. 24:21; John 12:25, respectively.
10 E.g. Mark 4:19 (although this represents a different Greek word); John 12:31.
11 E.g. Matthew 8:12; 13:50; 18:8f.; 22:13; 25:30, 41; Mark 9:43, 45; Luke 3:17.

Chapter 4

1 Cf. David Daube, *Rabbinic Judaism*, pp. 55ff.; David Hill,

Matthew, p. 117; B. H. Branscomb, *Jesus and the Law*, pp. 227ff.

2 Cf. A. H.McNeile, *Matthew*, p. 58; Tasker, *Matthew*, pp. 65f. *et al.*

3 D. A. Carson, *Commentary on Matthew* (The Expositor's Bible Commentary, ed. Frank E. Gaebelein, Zondervan, Grand Rapids, 1983), *ad. loc.* I had the privilege of reading much of this in draft, but Dr Carson may have made minor changes in the published version which is not yet in print.

4 Although Daube goes on to say that the Rabbis, in practice, often used this form of argument to combat an interpretation maintained by others and to 'substitute a new, freer meaning' (*Rabbinic Judaism*, pp. 57ff.).

5 Cf. Banks, *Jesus and the Law*, p. 191 (my italics).

6 Ex. 20:7, 16; Deut. 5:11, 20; cf. Lev. 19:12.

7 Cf. Num. 30:2; Deut. 23:21.

8 Cf. Rom. 1:9; 2 Cor. 1:23; 1 Thess. 2:5, 10.

9 Although, it seems, no such teaching can be found in the rabbinic literature that has come down to us. Cf. C. G. Montefiore, *The Synoptic Gospels*, II, pp. 78ff.

10 Cf. Luke 13:13; Mark 1:21 ff.; Luke 14:1ff.; John 5:1ff.; John 9:1f.

11 But there is strong manuscript evidence for reading 'son' rather than 'donkey' in Luke 14:5.

12 This is remarkably similar (in its basic concept of an approach to God, in some of its legal results and in the purposes for which it was used) to the Islamic *waqf* (a special form of endowment or 'trust').

13 Cf. Matt. 9:25; Matt. 8:3; Matt. 9:20 (with parallels in each case).

Chapter 5

1 Luke 6:20–49. There is no necessary contradiction if Matthew and Luke are, in fact, referring to the same occasion. 'The hill' in Matt. 5:1 probably means 'the hill

country', and this was not only composed of peaks! It seems, moreover, that part of the 'Sermon' (which, *if* it was given on one occasion, would have been wholly indigestible unless it was spread over several sessions) was given to a larger group than other parts; and this would suggest a plateau.

2 ‘"... As we forgive ...": A Note on the Distinction between Deserts and Capacity in the Understanding of Forgiveness', in *Donum Gentilicium*, p. 72.

3 Moule insists that the '*hoti*' (because) in Luke 7:47 depends on 'I tell you', rather than on 'have been forgiven' (p. 74).

4 Matt. 18:15ff. – but it is far from easy to see how this principle could be effectively applied in many situations today.

5 For an explanation of a statement that at first sight seems to be scientifically impossible, cf. John Stott, *Counter-culture*, p. 60.

6 Although there may also be a reference to the fact that in heaven the justice denied on earth will indeed obtain.

Chapter 6

1 Mark 12:17; Matthew 22:21; Luke 20:25.

2 Cranfield, *Mark* p. 369. Cf. also B. H. Branscomb, *Mark*, p. 213; D. E. Nineham, *Mark*, p. 314.

3 Matt. 22:19; Luke 20:24; Mark 12:15.

4 These were stamped with flowers, etc.

5 Cf. E. Stauffer, *Caesars*, pp. 124ff.; E. Schweizer, *Mark*, p. 244.

6 R. J. Cassidy, *Jesus*, p. 163.

7 Flavius Josephus, *Jewish War* vii. vi. 6. (Cf. Hill, *Matthew*, p. 272).

8 It is, however, possible that Paul regarded *any* act of inter-course as involving a union which was more than purely physical. So if (as has been suggested) the prostitute

concerned would quite probably have been a 'vestal virgin' of Aphrodite, the stark anomaly of one who belonged, body and soul, to Christ making himself in any way one with such a woman and her goddess is even more obvious.

9 By 'today' I deliberately exclude from discussion 'levirate marriages', polygamous marriages and unions with slave concubines in the Old Testament, or polygamous marriages contracted in various cultures today prior to conversion.

10 To define these terms adequately is not practicable in this context.

11 As distinct from civil law.

12 Contrast Islamic law, which permits a husband who has divorced his wife by a 'triple' repudiation to remarry her *only* if she has first been married to another man, and then again been divorced (or widowed). This has led to a practice which Muhammad certainly did not envisage.

13 It has been suggested that the Greek word *porneia* might have other meanings in the N.T. (e.g. Acts 15:20); but these would seem largely irrelevant in this context.

14 Cf. Matt. 5:32; 19:9; Mark 10:11; Luke 16:18.

15 Cf. Mark 10:12. E.g. Herodia. In contemporary Roman law the wife could also divorce her husband, and Mark's Gospel was almost certainly written for the Church in Rome. But cf. Lane (*Mark,* p. 352) for the variant readings in this verse.

16 Nor is there any necessary contradiction between 1 Corinthians 7:10f and Matthew 5:32 and 19:9. Paul was, it seems, dealing with specific questions, and was not contemplating the special case raised by adultery.

17 On the traditional interpretation, the commendation was, of course, for his 'prudence', not his morality! Cf. J. Duncan M. Derrett, *Law,* pp. 48-78.

18 Although this does not necessarily mean that *appropriate* self-defence is excluded in all circumstances.

19 'L'Épée de Jésus', in *Nouvelle revue française* 1966, quoted in English by Jacques Ellul, *Violence* (SCM, London, 1970), p. 47.

Chapter 7

1 C. K. Barrett, *Gospel,* pp. 41ff.
2 Cf. T. W. Manson, *Teaching,* p. 227; Moule, *Christology,* p. 14.
3 'The Historic Problem of the Death of Jesus', *More Studies,* p. 99.
4 Cf. R. Otto, *Kingdom,* pp. 227f. But I do not agree with his insistence that the words 'you will see' must have meant that the members of the Sanhedrin would themselves live to see the Parousia. (In this context cf. Cranfield, *Mark,* 445).
5 This is explicit, in Jesus' own words, in Mark 13:32. But it is also inherent in the fact that he was truly 'made man', with a human mind and psyche as well as body. Cf. Luke 2:52; Heb. 2:10, 17; 4:15; 5:7.
6 Literally, 'God is Salvation'.
7 Cf. Vincent Taylor, *Sacrifice,* pp. 193f.; W. Zimmerli and J. Jeremias, *Servant,* pp. 101f.
8 Hooker, *Servant,* pp. 74ff.; Barrett, 'Mark 10:45', in *N. T. Essays,* pp. 1–18.
9 Cf. O. Cullmann, *Christology,* p. 65 (with pp. 55 and 60–9).
10 R. T. France, *Jesus,* p. 118.
11 Cf. 1 Cor. 11:25 – a record of the same tradition committed to writing at what was probably an even earlier date.
12 Even W. G. Kümmel, *Promise,* p. 73, concedes that in this verse 'doubtless ideas of Isa. 53 are to be found'.
13 Cf. John Brown, *Hebrews,* pp. 438–43; A. B. Bruce, *Hebrews,* pp. 378-81.

Chapter 8

1 Cf. George Johnston, *The Spirit-Paraclete in the Gospel of John.*
2 Cf. R. M. Wilson, *The Gentiles and the Gentile Mission in Luke-Acts, passim.*
3 Cf. J. Jeremias, *Jesus' Promise to the Nations,* pp. 42f.

4 Rather than 'doublets', these stories are probably variants on the same basic theme, told by Jesus on different occasions in his itinerant ministry.

5 Cf. Gal. 4:21–31, Heb. 4:22ff. and Acts 15:16ff., for example. But comment on these passages falls outside the scope of this book.

6 Cf. A. L. Moore, *Parousia*, pp. 141f., and Matthew's use of *ap' arti* in 23:39 and 26:29. Cf. also Cranfield, *Mark*, pp. 444f.

7 It is possible that Luke amplified Mark's cryptic reference in the light of history. But this is by no means a necessary inference. Thus Caird remarks (1) that 'none of the distinctive features of the siege as it is described by Josephus are found here; the language of the passage is drawn from Old Testament prophecies and descriptions of the fall of Jerusalem in 586 B.C.'; and (2) that 'there can be no doubt that Jesus repeatedly foretold the violent end to which Jerusalem was hastening' (*Luke*, p. 231).

8 Cf. Marshall, *Luke*, p. 780.

9 W. Michaelis, quoted by W. G. Kümmel, *Promise*, p. 61.

10 H. Conzelmann, *The Theology of St Luke*, pp. 104f.

11 Cf. Tasker, *Matthew*, p. 42.

12 Cf. Moore, *Parousia*, pp. 143ff.

13 David Wenham, '"This generation will not pass ..." A study of Jesus' future expectation in Mark 13', in *Christ*, pp. 127–37.

14 For apostolic teaching on this subject, cf. especially 1 Thess. 4:15–18.

15 These words provide support for Paul's doctrine of justification by faith, since 'justification', in this sense, means a verdict of acquittal on the Day of Judgment. This future verdict is then predicated, and its consequences experienced, here and now (cf. Barrett, *Romans*, pp. 74ff.)

16 Or even, as Hill suggests, 'characteristic of the Age to come' (*Matthew*, p. 331).

17 Cf. Matt. 3:12; 8:12; 13:42; 18:8.

18 Article on 'Eschatology' in *The Illustrated Bible Dictionary*, Vol. I, p. 475.

19 Cf. Matt. 10:22; 24:13, 42–7; Mark 13:33–7; Luke 12:35–48; 21–34ff.

Epilogue

1 Cf. G. Vermēs, *Jesus*, pp. 195f.
2 Cf. the very cautious assessment in J. D. G. Dunn, *Christology*, pp. 26f.
3 Although some people's conscious experience comes, no doubt, in the reverse order: a knowledge of God as Father, followed by a growing realisation of the implications of his kingly rule.

List of Authors Cited

Banks, Robert, *Jesus and the Law in the Synoptic Tradition* (CUP, Cambridge, 1975).

Barclay, William, *The Mind of Jesus* (SCM, London, 1967).

Barrett, C. K., *A Commentary on the Epistle to the Romans* (Adam & Charles Black, London, 1957).

Jesus and the Gospel Tradition (SPCK, London, 1967).

The Gospel according to St John (2nd edn., SPCK, London, 1978).

'The Background of Mark 10:45', in *New Testament Essays* (ed. A. J. B. Higgins, Manchester University Press, Manchester, 1959).

Bauckham, R. J., 'Eschatology', in *The Illustrated Bible Dictionary* (IVP, Leicester, 1980).

Bell, Richard, *Introduction to the Qur'ān* (University Press, Edinburgh, 1953).

Bornkamm, Günther, *Jesus of Nazareth* (Hodder & Stoughton, London, 1960).

Bouyer, L. *Le Fils éternal: Théologie de la Parole de Dieu et Christologie* (Cerf, Paris, 1974), quoted in English by Mascall, E., *Theology and the Gospel of Christ* (SPCK, London, 1977).

Branscomb, B. H., *Jesus and the law of Moses* (Hodder & Stoughton, London, 1930).

The Gospel of Mark (Hodder & Stoughton, London, 1931).

Bright, John, *The Kingdom of God* (Nashville, Abingdon, 1953).

Brown, John, *The Epistle to the Hebrews* (ed. David Smith, Banner of Truth, London, 1961).

Bruce, A. B., *The Epistle to the Hebrews* (T. & T. Clark, Edinburgh, 1899).

Caird, G. B. *The Gospel of Luke* (Adam & Charles Black, London, 1963).

The Language and Imagery of the Bible (Duckworth, London, 1980).

Carmichael, Joel, 'L'Epée de Jésus', in *Nouvelle revue française*, 1966, quoted in English by Ellul, J., *Violence* (SCM, London, 1970).

Carson, D. A., *Commentary on Matthew* (Zondervan, Grand Rapids, 1983).

N.B. See note 3 to my chapter 4.

Cassidy, R. J., *Jesus, Politics and Society* (Orbis Books, New York, 1973).

Conzelmann, H., *The Theology of St Luke* (E. T., Faber & Faber, London, 1960).

Coulson, N. J., *A History of Islamic Law* (University Press, Edinburgh, 1964).

Cranfield, C. E. B., *The Gospel according to St Mark* (CUP, Cambridge, 1959).

Cullmann, Oscar, *The Theology of the New Testament* (E.T., SCM, London, 1959).

'The Return of Christ', in *Early Church* (ed. A. J. B. Higgins, SCM, London, 1956).

Curtis, W. A., *Jesus Christ the Teacher* (OUP, Oxford, 1943).

Dalman, G., *Jesus-Jeshua* (E.T., SPCK, London, 1929).

Daube, David, *The New Testament and Rabbinic Judaism* (Athlone Press, London, 1956).

Davies, W. D., *The Setting of the Sermon on the Mount* (CUP, Cambridge, 1964).

Derrett, J. D. M., *Law in the New Testament* (Darton, Longman and Todd, London, 1970).

Dodd, C. H., *The Parables of the Kingdom* (Nisbet, London, 1935).

'The Fall of Jerusalem and the "Abomination of Desolation"', in *JRS*, 37, 1947.

'The Historical Problem of the Death of Jesus', in *More New Testament Studies* (Manchester University Press, Manchester, 1968).

'A Hidden Parable in the Fourth Gospel', in *More New*

Testament Studies (Manchester University Press, Manchester, 1968).

Dunn, J. D. G., *Christology in the Making* (SCM, London, 1980).

Ellis, E. Earle, *The Gospel of Luke* (Revised, Oliphants, London, 1974).
Prophecy and Hermeneutic (J. C. B. Mohr, Tübingen, 1978).

Ellul, Jacques, *Violence* (SCM, London, 1970).

France, R. T., *Jesus and the Old Testament* (Tyndale Press, London, 1971).
'The authenticity of the sayings of Jesus', in *History, Criticism and Faith* (ed. Colin Brown, IVP, Leicester, 1976).

Galot, J., *La Personne du Christ* (Duculot, Gambloux, and Lethielleux, Paris, 1969), quoted in English in Mascall, E., *Theology and the Gospel of Christ* (SPCK, London, 1977).

Gerhardsson, Birger, *Tradition and Transmission in Early Christianity* (CWK, Gleerup, Lund, 1964).

Green, Michael, *I Believe in Satan's Downfall* (Hodder & Stoughton, London, 1981).

Guthrie, Donald, *New Testament Theology* (IVP, Leicester, 1981).

Hendriksen, W. *Gospel of Matthew* (Banner of Truth, London, 1974).

Hill, David, *The Gospel of Matthew* (Oliphants, London, 1972).

Hooker, Morna, *Jesus and the Servant* (SPCK, London, 1959).

Hoskyns, E. C., *The Riddle of the New Testament* (Faber & Faber, London, 1931).

Houlden, J. L., *Ethics and the New Testament* (Mowbrays, London, 1973).

James, M. R., *The Apocryphal Gospels* (Clarendon Press, Oxford, 1924).

Jeffery, Arthur, *The Qur'ān as Scripture* (Russell Moore, New York, 1952).

Jeremias, Joachim, *Jesus' Promise to the Nations* (E.T., SCM, London, 1958).

The Parables of Jesus (E.T., Revised edn., SCM, London, 1963).

The Prayers of Jesus (E.T., SCM, London, 1967).

Jeremias, J. and Zimmerli, W., *The Servant of God* (E.T., Revised, SCM, London, 1965).

Johnston, George, *The Spirit-Paraclete in the Gospel of John* (CUP, Cambridge, 1970).

Josephus, Flavius, *Jewish War.*

Klausner, Joseph, *Jesus of Nazareth* (Allen and Unwin, London, 1925).

Kümmel, W. G., *Promise and Fulfilment. The Eschatological Message of Jesus* (E.T., SCM, London, 1957).

Ladd, G. E., *The Presence of the Future* (Eerdmans, Grand Rapids, Michigan, 1974; SPCK, London, 1980).

Lane, W. L., *The Gospel according to Mark* (Eerdmans, Grand Rapids, Michigan, 1974).

Lightfoot, R. L., *St John's Gospel* (ed. C. F. Evans, Clarendon Press, Oxford, 1956). Now OUP paperback, Oxford, 1960.

Lloyd-Jones, Martyn, *Studies in the Sermon on the Mount* (Inter-Varsity Fellowship, London, 1959).

McNeile, A. H., *The Gospel according to St Matthew* (Macmillan, London, 1915).

Manson, T. W., *The Teaching of Jesus* (CUP, Cambridge, 1951).

'The Cleansing of the Temple', in *B.J.R.L.*, 33, 1950–1.

Marsh, John, *Saint John* (Penguin Books, Middlesex, 1968).

Marshall, I. H., *The Gospel of Luke* (Paternoster Press, Exeter, 1978).

I Believe in the Historical Jesus (Hodder and Stoughton, London, 1977).

New Testament Interpretation (ed. I. H. Marshall, Paternoster Press, Exeter, 1977).

Montefiore, C. G., *The Synoptic Gospels* (Macmillan, London, 1927).

Moore, A. L., *The Parousia in the New Testament* (Brille, Leiden, 1966).

Morris, Leon, *The Gospel according to Luke* (IVP, London, 1974).

Moule, C. F. D., *The Phenomenon of the New Testament* (SCM, London, 1967).

The Origin of Christology (CUP, Cambridge, 1977).

'Mark 4:1–20, Yet once more', in *Neotestamenta et Semitica* (ed. E. Earle Ellis and Max Wilcox, T. & T. Clark, Edinburgh, 1969).

'"... As we forgive ...". A Note on the Distinction between Deserts and Capacity in the Understanding of Forgiveness', in *Donum Gentilicium* (ed. E. Bammel *et al.*, Clarendon Press, Oxford, 1978).

Nineham, D. E., *The Gospel of St Mark* (Adam & Charles Black, London, 1963).

Nixon, Robin, Matthew, in *The New Bible Commentary Revised* (ed. D. Guthrie and J. A. Motyer, IVP, London, 1970).

Otto, Rudolf, *The Kingdom of God and the Son of Man* (E.T., Revised edn., Lutterworth, London, 1943).

Plummer, Alfred, *An Exegetical Commentary on the Gospel according to Matthew* (Robert Scott, London, 1951).

Ramsey, A. M., *The Resurrection of Christ* (Geoffrey Bles, London, 1945).

Riesenfeld, Harald, *The Gospel Tradition* (Blackwell, Oxford, 1970).

Roberts, C. H., *An Unpublished Fragment of the Fourth Gospel* (Manchester University Press, Manchester, 1935).

Robinson, J. A. T., *Redating the New Testament* (SCM, London, 1976).

Sanders, E. P., *The Tendencies of the Synoptic Gospels* (CUP, Cambridge, 1969).

Schacht, Joseph, *Origins of Islamic Jurisprudence* (Clarendon Press, Oxford, 1950).

Schürer, Emil, *A History of the Jewish People in the Time of Christ* (New E.V., Vol. II, ed. G. Vermēs, F. Miller and M. Black, T. and T. Clark, Edinburgh, 1979).

Schweizer, E., *The Good News according to Mark* (SPCK, London, 1971).

Stanton, G. N., *Jesus of Nazareth in New Testament Preaching* (CUP, Cambridge, 1974).

Stauffer, E., *Christ and the Caesars* (SCM, London, 1955).

Stott, John R. W., *Christian counter-culture* (IVP, Leicester, 1978).

Tasker, R. V. G., *The Gospel according to St John* (Tyndale Press, London, 1960).
The Gospel according to St Matthew (Tyndale Press, London, 1961).

Taylor, Vincent, *The Gospel according to St Mark* (2nd edn., Macmillan, London, 1966).
Jesus and his Sacrifice (Macmillan, London, 1959).

Temple, William, *Readings in St John's Gospel* (Macmillan, London, 1942).

Torrance, T. F., Foreword to *Christ's Words* (British and Foreign Bible Society, London, 1980).

Tozer, A. W., *The Pursuit of God* (Marshall, Morgan and Scott, London, 1961).

Vermēs, G., *Jesus the Jew* (Collins, London, 1973).

Wenham, David, '"This generation will not pass . . ." A study of Jesus' future expectation in Mark 13', in *Christ the Lord* (ed. H. H. Rowdon, IVP, Leicester, 1982).

Whale, J. S., *Christian Doctrine* (CUP, Cambridge, 1942).

Wilson, R. M., *The Gentiles and the Gentile Mission in Luke –Acts* (CUP, Cambridge, 1973).

Zimmerli W. and Jeremias, J., *The Servant of God* (E.T., Revised edn., SCM, London, 1968).

Index